Rawlins · Torrington · Mitchell
SCOTTS BLUFF · Scottsbluff
N. M. Cs
Hanna · Chugwater · Gering · Bayard

MEDICINE BOW MTS.

Saratoga
Laramie · Cheyenne · Kimball
Raggs · UP · 80

Walden · ROCKY MTN. NATIONAL PK. · Fort Collins · Sterling
Craig · Steamboat Springs · Eaton · Greeley
Maybell · Estes Park · Loveland · Brush
Oak Creek · Granby Lake · Longs Pk. · 76
Kremmling · Longmont · Fort Morgan · Aki
Meeker · Hot Sulphur Sprs. · Moffat Tunnel · Brighton · BN
Glenwood Springs · Berthoud Pass · Boulder · Aurora
Rifle · Wolcott · Central City · Golden · UP
COLORADO · Eagle · Mt. Evans · Denver
GRAND MESA · Breckenridge · Littleton
Junction · Mt. Elbert · Climax · Castle Rock · Limon
Aspen · Leadville · Fairplay
Paonia · Castle Peak · Mt. Harvard · Hugo
BLACK CANYON OF THE GUNNISON N.M. · Buena Vista · FLORISSANT FOSSIL BEDS N.M. · Manitou Springs
Gunnison · Cripple Creek · Pikes Pk. · Colorado Springs · Kit C
rose · Salida · Canon City
Uncompahgre Pk. · Saguache · Florence · Pueblo · Ordway · Las Animas
els · Ouray · Westcliffe · Fowler · Rocky Ford
ide · Silverton · Creede · GREAT SAND DUNES N.M. · La Junta
Del Norte · Center · Huerfano
SAN JUAN MTS. · Blanca Pk. · Walsenburg
Monte Vista · Rio Grande · Aguilar
Summit Pk. · Alamosa · Sp
Durango · Pagosa Springs · San Luis · Trinidad
Antonito · SANGRE DE CRISTO
N.M. · Chama · Raton · Folsom
ztec · CAPULIN MTN. N.M.
Tierra Amarilla · Questa · Des Moines
Taos · Wheeler Pk.
on · Pueblo · Cimarron · Springer · Clayton
Taos

ROCKY MOUNTAIN
HIGHWAY

ROCKY MOUNTAIN HIGHWAY

STORIES AND PHOTOS OF MY 25 YEARS
TRAVELING WITH JOHN DENVER

LOWELL NORMAN

With Contributions by Rush Evans

weldon**owen**

For Lane Taylor & Tyler Fielding

CONTENTS

Maroon Bells from Maroon Lake Trail in summer. Photo courtesy Lowell Norman.

"Bliss!" Photo courtesy John Denver photo archive.

PROLOGUE

It should have been an uneventful flight. We took off from Aspen around noon on a beautiful late-summer day. The skies were clear, and the winds were calm; the kind of day in the Rockies that makes you want to go fishing or hiking, a get-out-and-do kind of day. But my time in the mountains was over, and I was heading home to my sea-level life in California.

My boss, John Denver, decided to chauffeur me east to Denver's Stapleton Field himself, as he was eager for some alone time in his Cessna 210 and had an open day ahead of him. It was also a thoughtful gesture that spared me from checking in and sitting around the Aspen airfield waiting for the commuter flight to arrive. I was seated in the copilot's seat, while John's son, Zak, who couldn't have been more than five, and his nanny were sitting in the back.

The takeoff was smooth, and as we made our turn east you could see the high peaks of Maroon Bells and range after range of mountains beyond. As I settled in to enjoy the view for the hour-long flight, we climbed slowly to an elevation of about 10,000 feet, passing mountain summits that didn't seem all that far below us. All was smooth and quiet.

A half hour into the flight, we crossed a mountain range and came into a huge valley—it was like a big bowl with high peaks all around. The day had gotten warmer, and the air was less stable, so as we crossed the valley, we were hit with wild wind gusts. The plane began to bounce like a Jeep bumping along rocky roads. I was harnessed tightly in my seat, but the sudden air pocket drops and turbulence caused me to hit my head on the plane's ceiling.

The wings flapped like a bird's, and I began to get squeamish. It had gotten noisy in the cabin, the engine working harder and the wind whistling outside. John looked over and sensing my concern, yelled over the noise: "It can get a lot more uncomfortable for us before it ever gets uncomfortable for the plane." Somehow, that was enough to settle my nerves. It was crazy bumpy, yes, but just over the next ridge was the city of Denver and smoother skies. If the plane could take it, then so could I. It was just a matter of hanging on for a few more minutes.

And then as we flew over the last peak, there was the city, sprawled out before us like a big welcome mat. Our airspeed picked up as we began our smooth descent. I looked in the back seat and saw young Zak, who hadn't made a peep during the rough part of the trip, sleeping on his nanny's lap. For him, it was just another outing with Dad.

And for me, it was yet another adventure with my employer and friend, John Denver. There would be lots of them in the twenty-five years we worked and traveled together. Sometimes those days would be smooth as glass, and other times so rough I thought about bailing out. But even in difficult times, those of us who loved John, and believed in what he was about, had faith he would always pilot us home safely.

Because most of the crowd was already seated by midafternoon, Red Rocks concertgoers were treated to what became a minishow during sound check. Photo courtesy Lowell Norman.

INTRODUCTION

We Were Expecting You

I was twenty-two years old in 1973, fresh out of college and working at an audio-visual company in Los Angeles. I lived in a big house with seven roommates in Huntington Beach, and each one of us had a pile of LPs– an eclectic array of musical styles. Pop, rock, folk, country, surf—it was all there.

One of the roommates had a new album by someone I hadn't heard of before. His voice was pure and clean, a perfect match for the songs about the natural world he sang about. There were strings in some of the arrangements, which was different from what was being heard on the radio then. The singer couldn't be compared to anyone else. His style and message were unique.

The record was called *Farewell Andromeda*, an album full of songs that painted pictures in my mind as I listened. Indeed, the album cover itself was a beautiful piece of artwork that included an eagle, a deer, other wildlife, and the bespectacled mountain man singer. Who was this guy?

The title song was getting radio play at the time, and it was named for our nearest galactic neighbor, the galaxy that occupies space in the universe a mere two and a half million light-years from our Milky Way.

There was a warm feeling in the music here, in both the words and the melody. I was transfixed, so much so that I began to write out scripts of what

I would do visually with the songs I was listening to. It was the first time I had done such an exercise. Music videos were still almost a decade away, but I was an audiovisual guy and a visual thinker. It was how my mind worked.

I showed the scripts to one of my roommates. She thought they were good and suggested that I show them to someone. To whom? The artist? Fat chance. I didn't have a clue how to go about that, or how I would get my ideas in front of that guy on the record. So, I just put them aside.

Around that time, I found myself unable to work on a particular audio-visual job because I wasn't yet in the union. As a result, my employer was happy to lend me to another company for a project out on the road with some singer who had filmed projection in his show. This trading of tech workers between competitors was common in those days. It sounded like a fun project to me, especially since it involved visual content synched up with live music, just as I had been doodling at home.

The film footage did not represent a narrative to go with each song, but rather a means of taking the listener into the world of the artist. The concerts at my new temp job were happening in big cities, and the imagery would take the urban dwellers in the audience out of the city and directly into the mountains, streams, rivers, and skies of which the musician so frequently sang.

And then, as fate would have it, I discovered I'd be working for that guy, the *Farewell Andromeda* guy whose record had inspired my homemade scripts. It seemed an extraordinary coincidence, but in retrospect, perhaps not. Everything I had done to that moment seemed like an education—and an opportunity—to get me to this moment.

So, I boarded a plane with forty bucks in my pocket. No credit card, no traveler's checks. I was headed to join the concert tour and flew to Ohio for one show at Blossom Music Center, just outside of Akron. Now twenty-three, I figured if anything went wrong, I'd just settle down in Ohio, since I had no way back.

Blossom Music Center was in the village of Cuyahoga Falls, which bordered Kent. I mention this to put a political context to my story. It was at Kent State University three years earlier, on May 4, 1970, when members of the Ohio National Guard fired into a crowd of demonstrators with live ammunition, killing four and wounding nine Kent State students. When I

John in the studio recording the vocal tracks for his *Earth Songs* album. Photo courtesy Janel Pahl.

first started traveling with John, the Vietnam War, although winding down, was still in operation. American boys were being killed while the North Vietnamese and American diplomats were arguing over a peace settlement in Paris—an argument then in its second full year. It would be another year before President Nixon resigned. Campus demonstrations against the war, mostly aimed at Nixon and his stubborn policy of "peace with honor," were still front-page news.

If you lived through those years and the political uncertainties and turmoil of that time, with all the strident voices shouting over each other, it's not hard to see how a generation took to one young tenor voice that carried a similar message and warning, but with a tone that rose above because it was softer and truer. John spoke the same message at that time and in that place, but in terms that were easier to hear and absorb. Now, at this first show in Cuyahoga Falls, the audience would be young adults, mostly students from nearby Kent State University.

When I got to the Holiday Inn, I started looking for my contact, tour manager Kris O'Connor. Walking down the hallway, I passed a man who looked like a musician and asked him if he happened to know where Kris O'Connor might be.

He said, "Yeah, he's right in this room right here. You must be Lowell. We were expecting you. Do you want to go miniature golfing with us? We'll get something to eat later. I'm John."

It was both an introduction and demonstration of exactly who John Denver was: friendly, unpretentious, extroverted, a little childlike, and easy to get to know. I liked him immediately.

John was famous on the radio but not yet on television, so no one recognized him—not even me, who only knew him from the art on the front of *Farewell Andromeda*. In those days he could go through an airport just like anyone else. It wouldn't be long before that would change.

John led me into the hotel room where the band was rehearsing. The air was thick with smoke from a joint being passed around—a fitting first moment in the music business. A few minutes later, we were all packed in a station wagon on our way to play miniature golf and find someplace to eat. It seemed I was already part of the family.

This is the way it was. If John liked you, he had a way of including you and making you feel like you were important—part of something bigger. He might have written the songs and sung them from center stage, but we were all part of the mission to deliver the music and its message to anyone who wanted to hear it.

The travel group at that time was small: John, tour manager Kris O'Connor, guitarist Steve Weisberg, bass player Dick Kniss, and me. Sometimes soundman Ernie Zeilinger would travel with us, and that was it. Six guys.

By the way, another part of being inducted into the family was getting a road nickname. Kris passed these out, and everyone had one. Steve was "Pokey," Dick was "Uncle Dick," and mine was "El Dub" (short for LW—Lowell, get it?). John was usually "JD" or "Junior." After I was christened with the El Dub nickname, it was rare to hear my actual name out loud. I was treated as a member of the band, and that's how it would remain when it came to traveling on the musical road I called the Rocky Mountain Highway.

This was the start of my lifelong adventure with John Denver. He would take me to places much greener and more beautiful than the plastic carpeting and little windmills at the miniature golf course outside Akron. There would be mountains, trees, forests, and the jungle lands of every city and concert hall he and our company would play. There would also be adventures, from filming humpback whales to exploring the ancient ruins of Mesa Verde (and, on a video shoot in Africa, having a gun pointed at my head more than once).

Woven through it all was the music and personality of John Denver, a man who transcended his time. The subject matter of his songs alone makes them relevant to future generations concerned about saving the planet. His shows were aspirational for a better world and inspirational for each person who was moved by his music. My stories of our adventures might be from a different era, but I believe the telling of them will bring you a glimpse into a simpler and gentler time. A time when a man's passionate songs of a better world were celebrated and revered.

You already know the songs. Now here are some stories and pictures to further illuminate the legacy of a world citizen I once knew and who the world celebrated as a singer of songs of nature and hope.

John during sound check somewhere during our 1980 Japanese tour. Photo courtesy Lowell Norman.

Chapter 1

LADIES AND GENTLEMEN ...

The stage is dark, save for a wash of dim blue light. Backstage, John stands alone in a corner tuning his guitar against a wall so he can clearly hear its tone. Everyone knows to leave him alone. This is his meditation before he walks on stage. The band gathers nearby. All is quiet. John hands the guitar to his equipment manager, Steve Voudouris, who will place it on the stage when the band enters. The house lights dim, John takes a last sip of tea, stands up straight, stretches his six-foot frame, and breathes, "Let's go!"

The band members take their places on stage first to subdued applause. They pick up their instruments and check their tuning. The crowd, anticipating John's entrance, begins to stir. The band stills and, a moment later, a voice offstage announces, "Ladies and gentlemen, Mr. John Denver!" The stage lights up in hues of orange and flesh pink, so bright you can clearly see the first few rows of the audience wildly cheering—many standing—as John takes center stage. A thousand cameras flash so fast they create a bright steady light, dissipating just as fast, giving way to the action on stage. John picks up his guitar, places the strap over his shoulder, leans into the micro-phone, and—over the cheering crowd—shouts, "Good evening, Atlanta!" He stands on a thick six-by-six-foot red Persian carpet with two monitors on each side, turns to signal the band, and strums the first few intro bars of "Starwood in Aspen."

The audience settles in for a night of musical and visual magic.

It takes a lot of work to make a show appear effortless. Just twelve hours earlier, two eighteen-wheel tractor-trailers pulled up to the backstage dock to set up for another show on our 1975 concert tour. Local union stagehands began the hours-long process of unloading and wheeling all the equipment onto the arena floor. In one truck is the "hanging system," a dozen or more large speakers, each as tall as a man. Two dozen smaller speakers are added and then tied together and hung from the rafters, angled so the entire audience can hear the same sound. The other truck contains all the concert lighting and set pieces that are wheeled onto the forty-by-forty-foot stage. PAR lamps are hung from an overhead truss supported by two towers that sit on either end of the stage. A large lighting control console is positioned in the middle of the audience next to the soundboard, where both will be manned by experienced techs.

Every concert has two separate sound systems—one for the audience and one for the performers. The more sophisticated system, oddly enough, is the latter. Each band member has his own monitor, individually mixed to what he needs to hear. For the bass player, the drums are loudest; for John, his voice and perhaps the piano are loudest, so he knows his voice is in tune. The audio technician controlling the monitor board has to mix the right sounds for each. During the show he stands at the edge of the stage and watches the band like a hawk for signals band members give him regarding the mix on their monitors. He is constantly adjusting to what they hear, but he never seems to have it quite to their satisfaction.

I arrive at the venue by midafternoon for my setup. Stagehands placed the three screens where the films are shown—the biggest one in the middle was fifteen by twelve feet. On each side of that screen is a stained-glass window piece and on the far edges are two more screens, each fourteen by ten feet. There are also plants dotted around to warm up the set and make it feel like you are in the living room of someone's home. John insisted on the plants being real, but they were always in some stage of dying, and we were constantly replacing them. Finally, we snuck some artificial ones in the back, and he never noticed.

I place the projectors, run the power to them, and fire them up to make sure they are working. (But I still have backups just in case one peters out during the show, which happened on occasion.) I run everything from a special console I had made, a white metal control board with tons of buttons that lit up like a Christmas tree and let me operate all the projectors from one place. I'm done by the time the sound check starts, usually around 5:30.

Like a well-oiled machine, my part of the stage setup is all very smooth. It wasn't always. My first day working with John about a year and a half earlier was also my introduction to the visual background show I was now responsible for. Background Engineers, the company that had originally sent me out to Ohio with John, had just retired an older gentleman who was having difficulty handling the workload. Kris O'Connor, John's road manager, had told the company, "Send a new guy or we'll find another vendor." My first concert would also be the first time I had seen the John Denver show. I understood the equipment and the concept, and I had a show list given to me by Kris that indicated the songs for which we had visuals, but the show itself was a complete mystery to me. I had not seen any of it, so I would have to learn about it in real time as it unfolded in front of ten thousand people, with only Kris in my headphones to coach me.

Behind John and his band stood three large rear-projection screens. Hidden behind these screens were three scaffold towers on which sat projectors. A large 16mm motion-picture projector was in the center, with slide projectors on either side of it.

My job was to set it all up, run it during appropriate parts of the show, and then, when the show was over, tear it all down, and pack it all up.

I was apprehensive about what surprises I might run into having never seen the show before, but Kris told me it was the smoothest they'd ever had. I'm sure he wondered if it was beginner's luck, or whether I just had a knack for it. The next concert would tell.

But my mind was at work on something else. When I got to that first show, I discovered my new adopted company's equipment was in horrible condition, and the quality of the visual effects were nowhere near the quality worthy of John's concert performance. I asked Kris if I could take the visuals home and work on them before the next show in San Bernardino, California, which was two weeks away.

He said, "Sure, do whatever you want with it."

This was my opportunity to both add my personal signature to the content for the visual presentation and to impress my new clients with my technical skills at creating a smoother presentation.

What I didn't realize is it would also get me fired.

The first thing I did in the two weeks between show dates was upgrade much of the slide show. I had been to the Sierras on backpacking trips where I had taken a lot of photos. I thought my scenic photography was more compelling than the images supplied for the show, so I added them. The second thing I did was contact a third-party vendor—actually, a friend of mine—to rent added projectors and dissolve units so that the slide portion of the show moved much more seamlessly.

I could have asked the guys at Background Engineers for the added equipment rental, but I knew in the back of my mind that they would reject it based on budget. So, I used my own money, betting that Kris and John would buy into it after seeing my version of the show, and that I'd be a hero. Well, I got it partly right. Kris and John did indeed like it much better and applauded my initiative and effort. Background Engineers, however, felt differently. I was called in to pick up my pay, which included a pink slip. My dream job working with a touring show full-time was over almost before it began.

I called Kris O'Connor and apologized for any issues my firing might have caused. He told me he was sorry to hear it and needed to call me back. I figured that was that, and I would never hear another word. Time to look for a new job.

Kris called me back within the hour and told me to wait for a call from Background Engineers. They called me moments later and said that perhaps they were a little hasty in firing me, and that I did do a good job for their client. They acknowledged that my heart was in the right place, but my actions regarding the renting of additional equipment from another vendor were both unprofessional and disloyal. I understood and agreed.

What had happened is that Kris had called and told them to hire me back or the John Denver show would go elsewhere. From there on in, I was treated less like a hired hand and more like a partner by Background Engineers. I continued touring with John under their employ for three more months, reworking and adding to the visual show, unencumbered by the rules and constraints of my employer.

At the end of those three months, on a flight back from a concert in the Midwest, John sat down next to me and said, "Come work for me." I would do what I was already doing and use the few months we were not touring to build our own state-of-the-art projection equipment. He promised to let me work on rebuilding the visual show with new motion-picture elements, larger screens, and more projection. It came with a monthly salary, so I would be paid whether we were on tour or not. I figured, for the first time in my life, I might be looking at a real job that could provide security for a year or two.

I took the show from three projectors to seven—six 35mm slide projectors and one 16mm movie projector—with photographic dissolves on the still-frame shots for six of the projectors, and film footage on the screen in the middle. Kris was knocked out. John, of course, couldn't see the presentation going on behind him as he sang. But when I showed it to him later at a sound check, he was as impressed as Kris.

Saying yes to the job offer was the easiest decision I ever made. And, as it turns out, the best. The photography I had been doing, the filmmaking classes I had taken in college, and the work for the previous employer all led to this perfect professional fit. It was almost magical. These days, I might have been referred to as a videographer, but that word didn't even exist then. I was shooting, editing, and projecting 16mm motion-picture film footage. The video revolution was another decade away.

While on tour I coordinated the visual effects; when off the road I purchased equipment and put together the next visual show. I was literally doing what I had been storyboarding at home while listening to *Farewell Andromeda* just a few months earlier. And, although I didn't know it, I would be doing those very things for that very singer for a very long time.

At this moment, though, I was satisfied seeing my part of this '75 show was ready to go. It was time for the sound check.

With the soundboard lit and all the techs in place, John and the band take their places on stage for a sped-up version of the show with only a few bars played of each song—just enough to check the sound of each instrument, test the microphones, and make sure the monitors are angled properly. If there are new songs in the show that night, or ones that hadn't been played in a while, they'll rehearse them. But once a tour started, the show's set list didn't vary much.

Once on stage for the sound check, John's routine is always the same. For him, disciplined preparation for the show is important, and those of us who work with him respect the regimen. If the sound check goes without a hitch, the band is offstage in less than thirty minutes.

After the sound check, John heads back to his dressing room. Somedays a massage has been ordered, other days he might play Ping-Pong for a while or just nap, followed by a long, steaming-hot shower while going through his vocal exercises. You can hear these from anywhere backstage: vocal scales and long tones, clicks and occasionally whistles. He then gives himself an old-fashioned shave, with a mug of shaving soap and a brush. He manages his dressing so there is no preshow time standing around in his concert attire, which is always a Western-style shirt by designer Anna Zapp, a pair of tailored dress slacks, and Western boots. He doesn't sit again until the show is over. On those days, John doesn't eat anything after breakfast and only dines after the performance. He begins sipping hot tamari tea with a bit of whiskey in it a half hour before showtime and chews several Fisherman's Friend herb lozenges before going out onstage. Fresh hot tea will be sitting on a stool there, along with more lozenges, a half dozen guitar picks, and the set list. He's memorized the songs and the order—the list is to remind him what guitar he needs for each. Circling the stool are a half dozen different guitars, a mandolin, and a fiddle. Like fine works of custom art, they nest proudly in their stands at just the right angle for John to grab in the low light between songs. At exact center stage stands his vocal microphone.

The lights from the overhead truss are now glowing with the spotlight on John. The bright wash on the band dims as my three giant screens light up with images. "Starwood in Aspen" is my first film cue of the evening.

From this first song, the audience is taken literally from the crowded streets of the city they live in to the peace and tranquility of the Rocky Mountains. By the end of this first tune and its accompanying film, John welcomes every audience member into his world—one of beauty, nature, and love of life. The highway to this magical place is the music; the vehicle you rode in is the film.

Latecomers aren't seated from that point until the end of his second song, "Mother Nature's Son," which also had film, bringing the audience further into John's world of the great outdoors. He doesn't want to interrupt the illusion the audience feels as it is being transported into this world.

Midway through the concert, the band takes a twenty-minute break off-stage. John, however, continues standing and performing the entire time—twenty-five to thirty songs total—without a break. Two or three times his tea is replenished by one of his traveling assistants or his road manager.

John's passion was communication, and that's what happened over the next two and a half hours between him and his audience. The sense of community that came from the show was what he liked best about music. He believed he was a messenger, that songs weren't so much written by him as they were interpreted *through* him. He felt he was simply a conduit for that which wanted or needed to be written. Some songs took months to complete or be fully received. Others came to him like a breeze. "Annie's Song," for instance, was conceived on a chairlift and completed by the time he had finished his ski run.

John wasn't alone in this view, as other songwriters have articulated the process in very much the same way. Legendary Texas songwriter Townes Van Zandt once said of "The Ballad of Ira Hayes" that he wished that one had passed through him instead of its composer, Peter La Farge. It's the idea that melodies and even lyrics are just out there in the ether waiting to be discovered by the songwriter. If true, then John surely tapped into some magical pathway, because he was writing great songs until the very end.

The encore was usually "This Old Guitar," a song whose lyrics were perfectly crafted as a personal thank you from John to the people who came and listened to him sing.

After the applause fades away, John walks directly back to his dressing room and changes out of his stage clothes. In later years, dinner, including a good red wine, was always waiting for him in the dressing room. By the time he was done with it, the stage was nearly struck and loaded back in the trucks.

Unlike Elvis Presley, who was already in a car being driven away while his audience was still applauding, John was more accessible. After he changed and ate, he would go out and greet the guests who were hanging out backstage, and he was pretty good at sticking around until everyone was able to enjoy a moment with him. We had three types of backstage passes on most tours: the permanent laminated badges worn by staff, the all-access stick-on pass for local crew and close friends, and the aftershow stick-on pass, which frequently went to the local promoters and members of John Denver fan clubs.

On some dates, backstage was nearly empty; on other dates it was packed with friends and friends of friends. The bigger the city, the crazier it was backstage. Many of his fans brought gifts for John, mostly artwork—the most popular being a portrait of John with an eagle or a hawk. I never knew what John did with them until I was in his home's wine cellar once, and I saw dozens of these stacked up against a wall. He never hung them on display, but he also clearly didn't want to just throw them away. He appreciated that a fan had worked hard to create it for him.

There was, of course, another category of fans—the obsessed ones. John's experience with overly zealous fans was probably mild compared to rock stars of the era, but there was enough of this behavior to be concerned. Security was important even for John.

Some of the female fans had visions and delusions that John was meant to be with them, and nothing would get in their way of making that happen. One of them somehow located my office in Tustin, California. She was so determined that she popped by every month or two in the hopes of seeing John there, which was ludicrous. John never had reason to visit my office. I went to him; he didn't come to me. I finally had to tell her that if she really wanted to meet him, she was in the wrong state. You just had to get rude sometimes. We would often get fans banging on the back door of the venues we played, hours before the show, who wouldn't stop until we opened it and asked them to. Then they would hand you an Instamatic, or one of those cheap throwaway cameras, and ask you for a picture of John. We were often obliged to take a picture, but it would never be of John, unless some random stagehand's name happened to be John.

Since I sat behind the giant screens during the concert to run the visuals, I used to get fans calling down to me from the upper decks before and after the show, always wanting me to get something signed or given to John. I never agreed to it. Backstage was already crazy enough. John wasn't really a fan of autographs anyway. In fact, for a period of time he flat out refused to sign them. He would nicely say, "No thanks, but I'll shake your hand." That usually satisfied the fan who just wanted some personal acknowledgment.

I was sitting next to John on a domestic commercial flight once. We were both dozing when I felt someone leaning over me. I woke up to find a man reaching over my aisle seat and me to nudge John. Not aware that he meant no harm, I pushed him back, which woke up John. Then the guy asked him to sign something for his wife's cousin or some such thing. John could have just said "no," but instead he grabbed the pen and paper out of the guy's hand, scribbled his autograph, and said, "I was sleeping." The guy apologized, and even though he got the autograph, I suspect he regretted that moment. This is why John always took the window seat with one of us between him and the aisle.

Occasionally people of celebrity status would hang out backstage to avoid the audience crowd while the house lights were still up. Then they would be escorted to their seats as the lights dimmed and the show began. Once at a show in Madison Square Garden, Robert Redford and his young family hung out with us for the hour before the show. He was the new hot movie star in those days, fresh off *Butch Cassidy and the Sundance Kid*. He and John had just recently become friends, the mutual bond being their concern for the environment. Redford and his wife and kids were nice, even a little shy.

I certainly understood why people as famous as Robert Redford needed an extra level of security when going out to a concert, but it was something that John rarely practiced. Maybe that's why he was so easygoing and friendly about meeting fans after the show. He genuinely appreciated them, of course, but he also believed that the more you connected with people by just fitting into a group instead of standing apart, the more you will appear to be a genuine person, which he was. When you act like a normal guy going about your business, people treat you less like a star and more like a friend. John was great at accomplishing this, and I think it's the big reason he was able to pretty much go and do anything he wanted without being bothered.

John was great at thanking everyone involved in a show from the stage at the show's end, and that always included me. His mentioning me by name led to it showing up in some of the concert reviews. My name had even turned up in a *Saturday Evening Post* article after my very first show with John in Ohio.

When I first started working for John, we would do three or four shows a week, so he could be home on Mondays and the early part of the week. These early shows were mostly college dates, some in the campus gymnasiums and some in theaters. College dates had an energy about them that other shows lacked. John was still relevant among the college-aged crowd. By the end of the 1970s, John was far more famous and successful, but his appeal now spanned several generations. To me, that mass appeal, coupled with his genuinely positive and aw-shucks nature, made him seem less relevant to the next round of young adults.

But in the first half of the 1970s, he was the guy from the radio who wrote and sang simple but brilliant songs with which many a teenager and young adult identified. Like his contemporaries, his songs had touched the younger generation by way of the radio, and those college kids were now experiencing his music in a fresh and personal way for the first time. They got it. And John certainly got them.

Even though John now had two massive hits, "Rocky Mountain High" and "Take Me Home, Country Roads," he still wasn't recognized in public. That early obscurity, however, was gone by 1975, after John started to show up on television. In fact, everything about John's life and music would change that year. Our road show would grow with his popularity. Our crew grew from the original half dozen to more than thirty-five people, as there was now a bigger band and a full orchestra onstage.

The crew was a small army of people who needed logistical help moving from place to place. Beginning sometime in the '70s, Englishman John "Clarkie" Clarke joined the crew as our logistical director. He worked with our tour director, Kris O'Connor, and Barney Wyckoff. Everyone's luggage was named and numbered, and we left it in Clarkie's care at the beginning of the tour and never had to mess with it again. When I got to the hotel, a little envelope was there waiting for me with a key or keycard. I would open the door to my room and there was my stuff, like magic. Clarkie and his small staff were magicians; anything we needed was possible with these guys. It was a big part of why touring with John was such a pleasure.

There was a professionalism that permeated the entire touring staff that started with Kris and Barney and trickled down from there. It really had to be that way, or it would have been chaos. We often occupied the whole floor of a hotel. By that time; these were four- and five-star hotels. My floor would often have a security guard parked by our elevator to protect who went in and out. Often a second guard would be assigned outside John's suite for added protection from overeager fans.

On that spring tour of 1975, we did roughly one hundred shows in ninety days, the logistics of which were ridiculous, but it could be done with the Starship. The Starship was a Boeing 720 former passenger jet, brightly colored in red, white, and blue, with John Denver's name now emblazoned on the side. It was lush and configured more like a party living room than a passenger plane, and was complete with a bedroom and a long bar. This was way better than flying commercial or in a small private Falcon or Learjet, as we had done before. It was how rock stars traveled, and that's what John Denver had become. Elton John, Alice Cooper, Bob Dylan, Deep Purple, the Allman Brothers, and Led Zeppelin had each occupied the Starship for major tours between 1973 and 1975. Zeppelin had just finished a tour with the Starship when we took it over on April 1, 1975.

That '75 tour was a big deal. Touring with the band was a first-chair musician from each instrument in the orchestra. Other orchestra players were picked up locally in their respective cities. A band called Liberty from Aspen was on the road with us as our opening act. Liberty would later be the long-term opening act for Steve Martin.

John always did great business in the South and the Midwest, but not as great in some of the major eastern cities. Washington, D.C., however, was an exception. At the nearby twenty-thousand-seat Capitol Centre, we held three sold-out shows in a single day: a matinee, an evening show, and a late show. Then we got on the Starship, landing in the next city as the sun rose!

We rode in Starship-style from April 1 through the beginning of June, wrapping up with three shows at the Forum in Los Angeles. The Rolling Stones took over the Starship a week later for their Tour of the Americas '75. I went through a difficult transition during this time; I'd gone from being one of six guys to being one of almost forty guys, making my working experience much less personal. I had been spoiled those previous two years with face-to-face time with my boss and an unhindered routine for making the visual part of the show happen. I was still only twenty-four, and thirty-one-year-old John Denver had already become a major musical celebrity during my short time with him. We were all dealing with the growing pains of his success in one way or another.

After two months off that summer, we put on a two-week string of shows back-to-back with Frank Sinatra at Harrah's Lake Tahoe in Stateline, Nevada. As a young guy and the product of the rock and roll era, I had never really understood the allure of Sinatra—until we did those shows with him. Like my boss, Sinatra was magnetic on stage, but he took it to a different level. I was there when he first walked on Harrah's stage in the early afternoon just to get a feel for it. That was kind of an interesting thing to do, given that he'd played virtually every kind of venue there was for five decades, but maybe that is one of the ingredients that makes a great performer: wanting to understand the feel of every room and stage. His crew had an old-school, standoffish, showbiz feel, a lot of aged suits around without much to do, but I found Sinatra himself to be a fairly personable guy. I didn't expect him to be so hands-on during setup but there he was, asking questions, under-standing where on the stage he could move, where the band would be and the piano placed, and how he would enter and exit.

We didn't actually perform *with* Sinatra; our shows were back-to-back in the same venue. Those shows went like this: A young, little-known come-dian named Jay Leno would open our show while diners finished their meals and the tables were cleared. Then ten minutes later, John would do the dinner show. The ballroom was then emptied and reset for the cocktail show. Then another comedian opened, followed by Sinatra, who would do the cocktail show to wrap up the night. At one of his first shows, guitarist John Sommers (who wrote "Thank God I'm a Country Boy") and I sat at a table with Milton Berle and former vice president Spiro Agnew, and their wives. That was the night I finally understood what everyone saw and heard in Sinatra. The command that he had over the music and his audience for those ninety minutes was just phenomenal to witness.

My longtime best buddy, Paul Arganbright, joined me as my assistant on those shows. Leno, Paul, and I became pals during that brief period. Leno was a lot of fun to be around, really grounded and without ego, just like you'd expect. After that first show, I came back several nights to watch Sinatra perform from the side of the stage.

We played at Harrah's Lake Tahoe three summers in a row, and then switched to winter dates to coincide with the John Denver Celebrity Pro-Am Ski Tournament, which was an annual televised special for John. During those summer shows, we played softball against Harrah's waiters, stagehands, and blackjack dealers; during the winter dates, we skied Heavenly Valley.

Actually, we played softball everywhere we went, even Japan. Leno was on our team at Harrah's, and Sinatra even came out for one of our games but didn't play. John was a decent athlete and always wanted to play left field. We always won, maybe because we were the best players or maybe because John was the headliner. We'll never know.

With television appearances, heavier touring, a larger organization, more recording, and two young children (Zachary and Anna Kate) at home, John was spread thin, and there was increasingly less personal time for him.

While the world was watching John Denver on television specials and guest appearances on *The Tonight Show* and hearing him on the radio, John was on the road, performing tirelessly from town to town.

With so much activity swirling around him, you would think John would be frequently drained of energy. We never saw it. We all called him the "Adrenaline Kid." He was inexhaustible. His boundless energy made all of us crazy at times, even those of us who were younger and presumably more naturally energetic. Only once do I ever remember him being so sick that he couldn't make a concert date, and that was in San Francisco at a private concert for the est (Erhard Seminars Training) people. He had to cancel because he lost his voice. He powered through everything else, always with a smile, always with a sense of mission and purpose.

During this time, with so much going on and his attention now so scattered, I began to feel less relevant to the organization. But John found the time for us to talk it through. "I got people pulling me every which way," he would say. "I can't possibly do everything that everybody wants me to do. I just do what I can. You just need to know that you're an integral part of what we do, and you don't need to worry about it." Well, I still worried about it.

After the '75 tour, my three-screen projection presentation was no longer part of a John Denver live performance, unless we were touring other parts of the world that hadn't seen it yet. In the United States, John's charismatic performance abilities drew many repeat customers. I would bet that more than half of our audiences were people seeing John for the second, third, or fourth time. They may want to hear those songs again, but maybe not see the same slides and film footage. I vigorously lobbied to redo the visual portion of the show to stay on, and we did make some changes. But for the next tour, he was going to go in another direction. Also, my part of the show took up a lot of room and ruined the chance of selling an additional couple thousand seats because my huge screens blocked the view of John on stage.

So, in '76, John did shows in the round, in which he took the stage to the center of the arena, and the audience surrounded the artist and band on all sides. This presented a problem and a benefit: There was no reasonable way to do anything visually, but at least all the seats in the circular arena could be sold to ticket buyers.

Although assured otherwise, I figured this had to be the end for me, especially as I was headed into a one-on-one meeting with my boss. But true to his word, John said he would keep me busy with projects. "I want to keep you on. I'm not gonna cut your salary or any of that stuff, but your job's gonna change," he said. "You're not going to go on the road in the US anymore because we don't need projection." He then started talking about his ever-growing cottage industry of activity and the wide variety of roles I could play in it.

He also set up a meeting for me with Jerry Weintraub, his dynamic manager, to see if any of the acts Jerry managed had a need for visuals in their shows. That meeting was when I first actually got to know Jerry. He sat behind his desk, a lit cigar in the ashtray, boots up on the desk, and told me showbiz stories for about an hour and a half. Little got accomplished other than Jerry becoming aware of the fact that I was ready and willing to work. Later he did ask me to help put together some visuals for Bob Dylan's live shows, but by then I had started a one-man production company for John. My work would expand into doing visual work with other bands, including films for Captain & Tennille, Seals and Crofts, and Three Dog Night. And there was plenty else to do for John: graphic design, album cover art, television special content, and a significant creative role within John's nonprofit, the Windstar Foundation.

And, of course, all the while taking photographs. A lot of photographs.

My access led to the thousands of photos I would take over the next three decades. Photography was not my job in the organization at first. The projected images were. I took the pictures for fun, and I took them everywhere we went. If I had two free hours in a new city or country, I would get out and explore, taking pictures along the way. We went everywhere, from the Sydney Opera House in Australia to Berlin, Germany, before the Berlin Wall came down. I captured it all. Plus, I took photographs of John. In doing so, I wound up documenting the richly diverse public, private, and musical life of one of the most famous and beloved entertainer of his time and helped create his image as an authentic and accessible man to millions.

On his Kawasaki traveling the back roads near his home in Starwood. Photo courtesy Lowell Norman.

Chapter 2

HIGHWAY CAUTION

"I've never known anybody who could bring the audience into the show like John did," remembered guitarist Steve Weisberg. "Listening to the music before I met John, I had decided I kind of knew who this John Denver was. He was gonna be a very average guy, pleasant, and that was gonna be about all of it. Well, I was very wrong. When Annie gave the eulogy after his death, she said it best. She said, 'John was a complex man who wrote simple songs.'"

Weisberg, who died in 2014 at sixty-four, reflected on our old boss in 2008, capturing a band member's perspective perfectly. "John understood people. There was a reason he took his time and introduced us one by one every night, including on *The Tonight Show*. John wanted us to feel respected, and he wanted us to have our own identities and recognition, as opposed to, 'Hey, how about the band? Now let's talk about me again.' Not that at all. Everybody got their moment. [Drummer] Hal Blaine had worked for everybody, but there were very few that he would metaphorically take a bullet for. But he'd take a bullet for John. And after me on guitar, James Burton. James would take a bullet for John. I doubt if it was because he was so knocked out by the complexity of John Denver's music. If you worked for John, you loved the guy, and you really didn't want to disappoint him because he made everybody part of this amazing phenomenon that was happening. Maybe it shouldn't be called a phenomenon. He expected it to happen. He made you part of it immediately. You just knew this is an uncommon thing. 'I am part of it, I am going to do my best.' He brought out the best in people."

When I joined John in 1973, Steve was on lead guitar, and Dick Kniss was on upright bass. It was a folk band in those days, all acoustic with John singing center stage with Steve behind him to his right and Dick on the left. John carried two guitars with him in those early years: a Guild six string and a Guild twelve string.

That was it. A year later John Sommers joined the band, adding banjo, mandolin, fiddle, and an additional guitar: a Martin six string.

A few months after Sommers arrived, Hal Blaine was added on percussion, giving the band more depth. Hal, as Weisberg said, had worked for everybody. A session drummer and member of the Wrecking Crew, he was the drummer on countless Top 10 tracks, from "Strangers in the Night" to "Bridge over Troubled Water." Hal was a great guy, but he tended to stay quiet and hang out in his room. He had a little drum pad, and wherever he was, he'd be hitting that thing. You'd have to drag him out of the hotel to do stuff. He'd already "been there, done that" for decades before working with the Denver show.

By the '80s, there were eleven musicians in the band and lots of changes were going on. Steve Weisberg was replaced by Herb Pedersen, Uncle Dick Kniss called it quits and was replaced by a series of bass players, including Emory Gordy Jr. and Jerry Scheff. Guitarist James Burton (now available since his days with Elvis Presley had ended) was added. Burton revolutionized pop and rock guitar playing, particularly on the early rock and roll records of Ricky Nelson. He also spent years on the road with Elvis fronting the TCB Band (TCB stands for "Takin' Care of Business"—a motto for Elvis and his organization). James was among the nicest people I've ever known. He was good and he knew it, but he didn't have a swollen head. He was a Louisiana boy of simple tastes with immense talent. He wanted to play guitar and do it with nice people making music he believed in—a perfect fit for the Denver show. James was discovered by Ricky Nelson when he was still a teenager, and he actually lived with the Nelsons in a spare room in their home during the first two years he worked with Ricky.

We talked about his time with Elvis a lot, and he wore his TCB necklace at all times. He wore it as a badge of honor. He was proud of his time with Elvis, and I know he enjoyed the openness he found in John, who interacted closely and respectfully with his musicians, as Elvis had. Also joining the band about the same time were Glen D. Hardin on keyboards and piano, and Jerry Scheff on bass—both Elvis alums. Legendary woodwind musician Jim Horn joined the band, as well as a group of background singers on many tours, each adding greater depth and diversity.

On the road, John was laser-focused on the show. Like Hal Blaine, he didn't get out and about much in the cities we would visit (with the exception of our softball games in the early years and his routine round of golf in the latter years). On the other hand, I had an inquisitive mind in those days and a lust to see everything I could in the time I had.

I figured this may be the only time I'll ever be in, say, Berlin, Germany, so I'd better seize the day and take it all in. Guitar and banjo player Herb Pedersen was a kindred spirit, so I often had a traveling pal. Herb and I were the only two guys on the tour who liked getting out and experiencing the cities where we found ourselves. While everybody else was still sleeping or just hanging out at the hotel, we'd get up in the morning, take a cab or rent a car, and go around town to discover what there was to see.

Herb was all about the music, the only guy in the band I knew who practiced his guitar every day. In fact, he actually called it practice. He had worked with many other artists before working with John, most notably the Dillards, Emmylou Harris, and Linda Ronstadt, and later, he and a former member of the Byrds, Chris Hillman, would form the Desert Rose Band. He and Hillman kept working together on the road well into the twenty-first century, and he's still out there making great music in the world of bluegrass.

I haven't talked to him in years, which brings up a good point about the road: It's like actors working together on a movie. Everyone gets super close for the common creative goal, but when the project is over, you lose touch after moving on to other tours, bands, and projects. I was something of a constant in John's world, but I sure saw a lot of great people and musicians come into and go out of our special inner circle. When you're in it, you just notice the camaraderie. We were a gang together. We would all pile into the same bus to travel from hotels to venues and back. We shared meals, good and bad. We were, for at least the duration of the tour, inseparable. Each of us was an essential piece of the John Denver concert puzzle. We loved that, and we respected each other. But when the tour was over, you went your separate ways, back to your real life and friends, and didn't talk much, even though many of us lived relatively close to each other.

Herb, as I mentioned earlier, replaced guitarist Steve Weisberg, whom John introduced on the great live album *An Evening with John Denver* as playing the "weird slide Dobro hubcap guitar," a description that captured an important nuance that made the Denver concert experience so special.

Steve remembered it this way: "That was just one of those Johnisms, him being himself, being endearing to the audience and coming up with that phrase, rather than just calling it Dobro, 'cause it *is* weird! It has in it what looks like a hubcap. It made sense and was one of the basketful of things that made the audience like him more.

"John was much more than a string of songs; he was a personality. What he did between songs was at least as important as the music. He made the audience fall in love with him. And he did it by being very accessible, normal—not aloof—and human. He'd joke around with the audience and make 'em laugh. He knew that if he makes them laugh, it relaxes them. And then when he wants to get serious, they're gonna be listening. In Madison Square Garden in the '70s, the backstage crew, the ushers, the ticket takers, every one of them would tell you that at that time, there were only two entertainers who could quiet and own the New York audience—the toughest on the planet—and they were Frank Sinatra and John Denver."

When auditioning for the band, John asked Steve what other instruments he played. "I said, 'Dobro!'" said Steve. "John said, 'Oh good, I like Dobro!' I had told a little white lie there. After he hired me, I went out and bought one. Dobro is easy to make a little bit of music with, if you're a guitarist. I'm far from masterful on Dobro, but I played basically in tune and found a part that fit well enough to make John want to put it on the record."

In 1974 we recorded *An Evening with John Denver* live at the Universal Amphitheatre in Universal City, California, which included a full orchestra accompaniment, arranged and conducted by Lee Holdridge. Lee is a composer and orchestrator John had met through his longtime producer and friend Milt Okun back when they were all working on Mary Travers's first solo album together (she of Peter, Paul and Mary fame). Lee had won a Grammy Award that same year for Best Original Score Written for a Motion Picture or a Television Special for Neil Diamond's *Jonathan Livingston Seagull* soundtrack. Lee worked with John off and on through the years, and he even wrote several songs for John, including a Christmas song recorded by John and the Muppets called "Noel: Christmas Eve, 1913" (with lyrics from a poem by Robert Bridges).

Lee brought another unique element to the John Denver sound, as popular music had rarely incorporated sweeping orchestral music into the arrangements.

"Folk music and classical music have always gotten along very well," said Lee. "If you go back to all the classical composers, they all borrowed folk melodies for their works. It's a very symbiotic style."

John loved what Lee brought to his music. "He always loved it when I put the orchestra behind him," said Lee of John. "He said, 'I feel like I'm floating on a cloud.' I tried to suit what I thought sounded good with the songs. I didn't really think of it as a style that I imposed on him. I would listen to the song and then I would develop around it what seemed to fit. The arrangements grew out of the songs. I would listen to his guitar, and I would hear a counterpart to it. I would sketch out an arrangement around what he had written, complementing his voice. I used the woodwinds and the French horns a lot, because they really went well with his voice, and the strings were great with his guitar."

There was an Aaron Copland or Americana feel to what Lee brought to those shows, which only made sense, given the material he was working with. "I kind of see John as a contemporary Stephen Foster," said Lee. "He hit that groove that Stephen Foster had hit in the previous century, where he wrote these songs that were very universal. It touched everyone. He came along in that same sense: very grassroots, very much coming from his folk background."

Lee's personal memories of John were much like those of the rest of us. "He was always very kind to me. He treated me well, he loved what I did, and I was always complimentary to him." Lee remembered when John first shared a new song about which he wasn't completely certain: "Annie's Song." When he first played it for me, he said, 'What do you think of this?' I said, 'That's a marvelous song. It's wonderful the way it is. We'll arrange it just the way it is!' But this seemed to concern John."

John's apprehension arose from the frequently frosty reception he received from the music press. "Critics would sometimes pick him apart for stupid things, and he'd worry about it," said Lee. "It would upset him some-times. He'd say, 'Is that song just not very good?' I'd say, 'They don't know what they're talking about. I live music. I know what I'm talking about, John. What you're doing is really good; don't worry about it.' He loved that I would always reassure him and confirm to him that what he was doing was good." John wasn't alone in questioning his talent. Insecurity seems to run deep with most musicians, regardless of their level of fame.

During the summer months, we put on a lot of outdoor gigs. Pine Knob Music Theatre (formerly known as the DTE Energy Music Theatre) was a particularly beautiful outdoor amphitheater that I remember well in Independence Township, Michigan, just outside of Detroit. We played a string of dates there in the late '70s and more in the years that followed. This was a projector show, so I was back in my old backstage setup, and it was from this viewpoint that I first saw a giant sea of cigarette lighters held high in unison at a concert during the singing of "Poems, Prayers and Promises." It was quite a sight.

Another particularly special outdoor venue was, of course, Red Rocks Amphitheatre. We always played there in the summer, and I was personally involved in those shows just a few times, as the visual show wasn't used every time John was there. Red Rocks is a stunning, historic natural amphitheater, one of the best places in the world to see and hear live music. It's just outside

Denver, Colorado, so it makes sense that John Denver is the artist most historically connected to a place of such natural beauty, and it's right there in his adopted home state. John performed there seventeen times between 1972 and 1989, and that's why his statue now stands on the premises.

For me, Red Rocks was a nightmare, professionally speaking. There was a natural wind tunnel within the barriers of the theater that turned my three giant film screens into sails. I had to put them up at the last minute before the show or they would blow away with the afternoon wind. We had one show for which we made the decision to not even attempt putting up the screens because it was so windy—they would have been torn apart. It wasn't a gig that I looked forward to in that respect, but make no mistake, the experience of playing Red Rocks was a lot of fun overall.

The view from the stage looking up was as gorgeous for us as it was for the audience looking down. And although not a great place for film projection, it was perfect for film photography. I took quite a few performance shots from the stage.

To begin our setup, we'd have to arrive early in the day, ahead of the fans. Back then, audiences were allowed to come in and claim the general admission seating in the afternoon. By 4 p.m., many of the ten thousand seats were already full. And that meant there was going to be two performances, as the early birds got to see our sound check. There was a rowdy vibe from the early arrivals that made it feel more like a festival event.

The average sound check ran about twenty minutes, and they were designed for just that: checking the sound. At Red Rocks, however, it was different. With most of the audience already in their seats, sound check became a full forty-minute matinee with complete songs, often featuring different members of the band performing a song solo.

Nowhere in the world is there a more perfect setting for a John Denver concert. And he loved playing there. His voice resonated beautifully off those red rock barriers, and a place of such natural beauty was also symbolically perfect for the man whose music was rooted in the celebration of nature.

As the breadth of John's live show expanded over the years, so did the number of his instruments. He went from those original two Guild guitars to a whole stable of guitars, each suited for particular songs. Here is just a partial list of the stage instruments he used over the years:

Guild F-50 six string
Guild F-212XL twelve string
1993 Taylor J15 Limited
Ovation Balladeer 1661 Sunburst
Yamaha L-53 #3 six string (twenty-one frets)
Yamaha 12 string
Fender American Vintage '57 Stratocaster
1979 Gibson "The Paul" Natural
Maton six string
Mossman Winter Wheat twelve string
Martin D-20 six string
Gibson ES-335 TD
Ovation Adamas 1687-9 (dark brown)
Ovation Celebrity CC-167 Sunburst
'70s Gibson F5 Mandolin
National Reso-Phonic Delphi Style-O Dobro
Ibanez George Benson GB10 N

In many cases, as with the Yamaha guitars, he owned several over the years. Toward the end of his career, he was playing a lot more with Taylor guitars, having all but ditched the original Guilds. Many of his guitars were used for just one song each. The Ovation Adamas, for instance, was used for "The Eagle and the Hawk" because it had such a full-bodied sound, and he could beat the hell out of it.

After John's death in 1997, mysterious things began to happen to his hefty collection of instruments. Some were lost during shipments, while others were stolen or misplaced during all the chaos surrounding his death and subsequent estate settlement.

Some years later, I was directing a series of children's videos for a music label when an executive from the company asked me into his office. He opened a guitar case and there sat one of John's six-string Yamahas. "Have you ever seen this before?" he asked me. "Looks like John's," I answered. "That's why I bought it," he said. "Nice find," I said, knowing it had gone missing months before.

John didn't trade in his guitars or sell them back to dealers; he either kept them or gave them away. So, I decided to do a little research on how this guy could have procured this Yamaha. I called Steve Voudouris, John's instrument and equipment guy. Steve said it had been shipped from Florida after a show and never showed up again. Someone had to have stolen it and sold it to a dealer in Los Angeles, where my friend purchased it. Other instruments ended up all over the country. I once got a call from a guy who sent me a picture of a guitar that was similar to one of John's Yamaha twelve strings, wanting me to authenticate it. I told him that I couldn't find a single picture with this guitar in it. He bought it anyway—for $45,000.

In the early years, John would do three or four shows at a time, followed by three or four days at home. This was a great model for him and fulfilled a commitment he had made to Annie, who didn't enjoy touring and rarely came along. This schedule wasn't as easy for me because I had to often fly on multiple planes from my home state of California to whichever city we'd be in. It was often a whole day of travel just to connect with the gang.

But for John, it allowed for the best of both worlds: family life and rockstar life. He had been very devoted to his marriage and family those first several years. But I noticed a shift in tone as the '70s came to a close.

John and Annie were unable to have their own children, so they adopted a boy, Zachary, and a girl, Anna Kate. The timing of his increased popularity and the required touring couldn't have been worse when trying to balance the demands of a young family. John was always a doting father when Annie and the kids were around. Their presence didn't change who he was, but they sure changed his focus. He was clearly an attentive father—as much as time would permit. And therein lies the problem facing every entertainer who is both married to his family and to his profession.

A concert tour is way more than a full-time job, and with television, songwriting, activism, and recording, John had other seemingly full-time

John on a summer day riding into Aspen in his Jeep. Photo courtesy Lowell Norman.

jobs too, all of which took a toll on him and his family life. Touring has torn many families apart, John and Annie's among them. John was surprisingly open, honest, and contrite in his autobiography, *Take Me Home*, about his marital infidelities on the road. John's brother, Ron Deutschendorf, once said, "When you're doing [a show with] twenty thousand seats, ten thousand of those seats are women who wanna be with you." That may be an exaggeration, but I was around John all the time, especially the first ten years I worked and traveled with him and the band. I saw little evidence of his transgressions, which tells you how successful he was with his discretion, making his later confessions all the more surprising.

For me, the young single guy, everything was an adventure, touring was fun, and I didn't face the familial separation that so many experienced. I was single my first six years with John, the most intensive period of traveling for me. Then, after I got married, I didn't go on complete tours, although I did do some of the big ones abroad like Japan, Australia, and Europe. Otherwise, I would fly in for a few days to take pictures at certain shows and venues. I had always loved touring, in general, but I also loved being a family man who was home more often than not.

John was a workaholic, and the rest of us had to be too, just to keep up with him. It was an exhausting task of re-creating an entire show in a new town every night, sometimes for weeks on end. Accordingly, John was good to his band and crew and afforded us first-class treatment, which was unusual at that time.

At the end of that tour in late '75, the one on which we had used the Starship plane (during which we had only two days off in April and May), we did a short tour of New Zealand, Australia, and Japan. He then invited the entire band to Hawaii for a week at the Mauna Kea on the Kona coast of the Big Island. Wives of band members were included, as was my girlfriend. It was an amazing week. We learned how to scuba dive and spent a lot of time diving off the coast of Kona. But mostly we ate and drank! It was a great way to wrap up an extraordinary year in all our lives. Then John went back to making records and television shows for a few months, and by March 1976, we were performing in England, followed by incessant touring for the rest of the decade.

I was always busy on tour. I had a lot of responsibilities and setup duties, so, combined with my adventuresome spirit, I was never bored and rarely lonely. But for those who were affected by loneliness, and regardless of how well we had it on the road, it was hard to escape. Loneliness can affect people in different ways, and its effects were significant for John, which I'm sure had something to do with the infidelities. It also had a hand in his drug and alcohol use. That just seemed a natural byproduct of life in a rock and roll band on the road in the '70s.

John had a squeaky-clean image both personally and musically, so it probably didn't seem to the public that drugs would be a thing in this organization. And it's true that we lived a different collective lifestyle from the traveling Led Zeppelin caravan. Regardless, they were still there.

In those early years of touring, John did have a hard-and-fast rule about drugs on concert days. Usage was strictly forbidden on show day. Period. The show was a sacred thing to him, and he felt a great sense of responsibility to the audience. I remember Steve Weisberg deciding that he intended to smoke weed as he saw fit, believing that it did not hinder his guitar playing during the show. When John got wind of Steve's philosophy on the matter, he fired him immediately. Steve was rehired an hour later, but the incident did reveal the seriousness that John felt about it. Others, who were not as open and honest as Steve, secretly indulged without John's awareness.

Drugs were never really an issue for John until we got to Australia, and that had nothing to do with getting caught with anything. It had to do with John honestly acknowledging at a press conference that he smoked marijuana. "Sure, I enjoy hash, I use it. I have a lot of fun with the stuff," John said, speaking to a particularly caustic group of reporters in Sydney. "But it's like alcohol. It should be handled with responsibility. You shouldn't let it get out of hand. You can get stoned on marijuana, but you can get high just being up in the mountains. I'm not suggesting that kids ought to use it, I'm just saying that I use it, and I don't figure it's doing me any harm. Everyone should make up their own mind on that sort of thing."

Tour management let out a collective gasp at this confession, and the cynical Aussie press took it and ran. Minutes after that press conference, every one of us still at the hotel got a call from Kris O'Connor: "If you have any drugs at all, anything you could get caught with—flush it down the toilet right now. Do not carry anything that could be construed as illegal on the remainder of this tour." We were all familiar with Paul McCartney's arrest at the Tokyo airport with pot in his suitcase. He spent nine days in jail, where he met someone guilty of the same crime who had already served seven years of hard labor. Although McCartney's fame would secure his relatively quick release, we couldn't count on getting the same treatment, and the disruption it would create could kill an otherwise profitable tour.

That evening's paper and the days that followed carried the story, and we were dogged by the press for the rest of the tour. That bad press out of Australia led John to call then president Gerald Ford and apologize for his behavior. To him, it was the right thing to do, as he was more than just a pop star by that time; he was also a public figure with a political voice and an increasingly literal seat at the table for cultural and environmental issues in both the White House and the Capitol (which would grow even greater during the Carter years that followed). Such access and influence that John so wholeheartedly welcomed carried with it a responsibility that he took seriously. Beyond that, he wanted to be taken seriously on his environmental work and his fight against world hunger. But if he came to be known as a druggie, he would lose all credibility.

Marijuana is now legal in many states in the United States, including John's beloved home state (the song title "Rocky Mountain High" was routinely used by journalists when the legalization news first broke in Colorado). John had quite innocently stated the fact of his usage, but this was 1976, and the world was not quite as ready or enlightened as he thought it was on the subject.

John's wholesome, clean-cut image was shattered, temporarily anyway, but it wasn't too long before it was restored. It seems the country can be very forgiving, as long as you're not a politician. Our entertainment icons seem to get a pass when any other public persona doesn't.

Life on the road is multifaceted. There's the performance side the public sees: big smiles, raw talent, and moments of connection through music. Then there's the side most performers and technicians experience: weeks or months away from loved ones when you can feel lonely in a crowd and temptations abound.

Aspen photographer John Russell shot a series of photos of John while my crew was setting up a commercial for recycled paper products. The results were some of the best and most used photos of John from the 1990s. Photo courtesy John Russell.

Chapter 3

ACCESS AND EXECUTION

My education in photography started the day my dad handed me his Pentax Spotmatic 35mm camera and explained to me how the relationship between light and shutter speed worked. The rest, he said, you'll figure out.

The first filming request from John came in the spring of 1974, when he asked me to come to Aspen to shoot film to accompany a song he was adding to the show. I asked him what he envisioned. He said, "Not certain. I just want to shoot some film up here while it's spring, but there's not really a storyline that goes with it. I just want something to support the song and take people where I'm thinking, you know?"

Basically, he wanted me to fly up to Aspen with all the professional motion-picture equipment needed to create a film montage (a music video, if you will) for this new song.

My dad had a credo he passed on to me, a remnant of his years surviving the Great Depression: "Say yes, then figure out how to do it."

So, I told John "Yes," as if it were a request I got every day. In truth, I had never shot with a professional Arri 16mm motion-picture camera before. I owned a Bolex 16, but it was a toy compared to what I needed for this shoot. I assured him that procuring the camera and gear and getting it all up there was no problem, but really, I had zero clue where to start looking for everything. In those early days with John, on the advice I had from my father, I said yes to everything, regardless of whether I knew how to do it or not. And I never asked about the details, like how to pay for all this! So now I was in a bit of a dilemma. Well, I figured, Dad got me into this by telling me to say yes to everything, so maybe he'll have an answer. As it turned out, he did.

The company he worked for, World Vision International, used media for various documentary projects, and they had an account at Birns & Sawyer, a film equipment rental house in Hollywood. I was able to order everything I needed on their credit, as long as payment was coming, which I assured them it would. I picked it all up, and the tech gave me about an hour's lesson on the Arri 16S camera, how to load the big 400-foot magazine with film (which you had to do blind in a changing bag), and all the other support gear.

I also had a book on using the Arri 16S, which I read cover to cover on the plane ride to Colorado. I was both excited and anxious about how the shooting would all shake out.

Successful photography, whether still or motion picture, is really all about two things: access and execution. The extraordinary access I found myself having all of a sudden took care of the biggest obstacle. The execution, that is the mechanics of photography, comes from shooting a lot of film. Executing good photography or filmmaking is really all about the way you set up images in the camera's frame. If you have an eye for photography, then you have the knowledge about how to set the frame that best tells a story. You are 90 percent on your way. The mechanical part can always be learned, but understanding the frame is where the art lies. You have to divorce yourself from all the other senses, like smell and temperature, and just concentrate on the image in the frame because that is the only story you will capture and the only experience the audience will clearly understand.

Because I had some experience with still photography, this part came naturally for me. It became habit—it was the way I looked at the world, with or without a lens. But the mechanical part of motion-picture cameras was not as easy. I was all thumbs at first, which I demonstrated on this first location shoot.

I got to Aspen late, and by the time I settled in my motel room, it was already close to 10 p.m. There was a message waiting for me that John and Kris would pick me up the next morning at 5 a.m. because they wanted to shoot at sunrise. I had no frame of reference at that point of what exactly we would be shooting, except I knew that it would be outdoors in the mountains. No script, no song lyrics. As the sky was beginning to brighten, we were traveling in John's Chevy Blazer and climbing higher and higher up around the mountains near Maroon Bells. Being a sea-level guy, now breathing hard at 9,000 feet, I was exhausted just dragging the equipment around, and the Arri 16S is a heavy metal tank, not to mention the tripod, fluid head, and bag of spare film reels.

As we traveled higher and higher in the truck, I finally heard the song we were using as our script. It was a song called "Spring," part of the "Season Suite" from the *Rocky Mountain High* album. My idea was to try to capture the sun rising on the first day of spring, the snow melting, flowers beginning to emerge from among the white pastures, the world coming alive with new growth and vitality. Simple.

We set the camera near a stream as the sun rose, glistening on the water's edge. The shoot was moving along nicely until about our third setup, when suddenly the camera began to make noises as if the film were not properly passing through the film gate. It was a problem with the 400-foot magazine that sat on top of the Arri 16S like giant mouse ears. It was not something I could fix sitting on a rock in a canyon. So, I improvised by taking off the magazine and loading the camera with 100-foot spools I brought along that didn't require the magazine. A 400-foot magazine of 16mm film is about ten minutes of running film. A 100-foot spool cuts that time down to about three minutes, but the upside is that they were designed to be loaded in light (a relic of the old newsreel days). The song was only about three and a half minutes long, but when you are shooting on the fly as we were without a script or even a shot list, I would burn up at least forty minutes or more before I had what I needed to edit down to a three- or four-minute film.

We shot what we could—and then I ran out of 100-foot film loads. We headed back into town to eat lunch and see if we could find more film. There were two nature photographers in Aspen, Mark and Marty Stouffer, who in later years would find quite a bit of success and fame with PBS's *Wild America*. I found them and asked if they knew of a source for the film or if they happened to have a spare Arri 16S to lend us.

They were happy to oblige, and to my surprise, even offered to help with the shoot. But John nixed this idea. He wanted us to figure it out for ourselves. Finding some film was okay, but he didn't want any other party involved. At first I didn't understand. Here were two guys willing to help us out; why wouldn't we take advantage? He explained it this way to his young, inexperienced photographer: "You're my guy for this. We need to be self-sufficient as a team. If I wanted those guys to help, I would have hired them in the first place. But I'm building an organization, and I want to do things our way using our people start to finish."

That was my first lesson in loyalty with John Denver. He would put all his faith in you to be left alone to do your job until he had reason to believe you were not capable. I realized at that moment that John had more faith in me than I had in myself. And I learned that loyalty was monumentally important to John. And John would remain loyal to me (and so many others, for that matter) over my entire career with him. By the way, I did figure it out. On the same trip, I had bought a book on lighting and another about that particular camera. I learned all I could, as my employer had quietly encouraged. We shot the rest of the needed footage with my camera, our way. We had lost a half day of shooting, but I had gained a valuable organizational lesson about working with John.

My job for the next twenty-four years, as it turned out, was to make sure I lived up to his faith and expectation in everything I was given to do. I usually did. But there were times I'm sure I didn't as well.

Considering all I was doing regarding the visual aspect of the show, becoming the tour still photographer was an obvious next step. And so, little by little, in that first year with John, I began to photo-document our tours. Over time, it was expected of me to have my cameras at the ready, and I was happy to do it, as it included me in a lot of situations I normally would not have been part of.

Being six feet six inches tall and somewhat lanky (not to mention shy), I had learned in life how to fold into a crowd without being too obvious. Other than playing basketball, I found little benefit to my height in those days. I hated the idea that I stuck out in a crowd. But now I found a certain utility in my height: It gave me a unique advantage for photography.

When crowds were present, for instance, I could easily shoot over their heads from a better angle. From the side of the stage, I could shoot over obstacles, speaker monitors, and lighting consoles. I could stay both out of the way and out of the audience's sight lines, while still getting good angles on John as he performed.

Part of that had to do with the way I shot. Of course, I never used a flash or strobe on any of John's concert shots, which meant I shot with the lens aperture wide open and with shutter speeds rarely exceeding $\frac{1}{125}$ second. I got away with this mostly because I knew John and his performance so well. I knew how he played his instruments and the cadence of his movements, having watched him so many times on tour.

I knew his rap, the pauses he would make between songs, the notes he would hold. Had I not, given the f-stops and slow shutter speeds I had to shoot (because I was just using available stage light), John would be nothing more than a blur on my Ektachrome. And don't get me wrong, in many shots he was. I'm sure I tossed out twice as many as I saved, and I've saved thousands.

I shot with 35mm Nikon F2s. I had two of them with motor drives plus a Nikkormat manual 35mm camera. The lenses I used most often for concert work were a Nikon 300mm f/3.5 fixed telephoto lens, a Nikon 200mm f/2.8 fixed telephoto lens, and a fast Nikon 85mm f/1.8 prime lens. I had an array of wide-angle and standard lenses, filters, and all the other goodies a photographer likes to have on hand.

I used a handheld spot meter to check exposures, as stage lighting would constantly be changing, although after years of shooting, you get to a point where you just know what will work. If a roll of film was used for a concert shoot, I generally pushed the Ektachrome processing one or two stops.

My first real photographic job (that is, a job I was asked to do apart from my normal duties) was shooting the cover for the *Back Home Again* album.

This is a great example of having access but not yet perfecting execution. The cover is of John and Annie sitting on his driveway fence. It's a terrible picture as Annie was squinting a bit, but she liked it better than the rest of the shots. Why? Annie had no interest in celebrity; it took some convincing to include her in the shot to begin with, and this particular shot looked less like her than the others. She really didn't want anyone recognizing her. At the back of the album was a shot of John and the band and all the family, taken next to his backyard pool.

John wasn't a big fan of posing either. To be honest, when it came to shooting portraits of him, he was a pain in the ass. He hated to pose because it didn't feel natural to him, and he usually saw no practical use for it. He didn't mind me documenting his comings and goings, concerts, even recreational times together, but he did not like to sit still for portraits.

I had sketched out the initial concept of this first album during an airport layover, a series of portraits arranged atop an antique bureau. The shot of John and Annie that made the cover was one of them. The design firm that was ultimately hired took the rest of the shots and stuck them on the inside album cover. In the end I got the photo credit, and an extra $2,500 for my effort. Not a big payday by today's standards, but a nice bonus then.

Because I always had a camera with me and took a lot of pictures, I became the de facto tour photographer. I didn't relish this second job. I had my duties setting up and running the visual portion of the show. During the songs that didn't have visuals, I would be set up somewhere onstage shooting photographs of John and the band.

When you're part of a group *and* you're the photographer, you kind of separate yourself from everyone. You become an observer more than a participant. Over time, you become the outsider looking in, which is essential to all photojournalism, to capture something that's real. If you immerse yourself in the story, it alters the story. The focus of your attention is through the lens of the camera, as you are constantly asking yourself what each picture is documenting, what each picture is saying.

I was an insider in some situations and an outsider in others. I was a little uncomfortable as an outsider. This was what I didn't like about being the photographer. The technical part came easy, but there was a lonesome quality about detaching from the group. What photography did for me later, however, was open another role in the organization, that of producing program booklets, promotional materials, and—later still—videos.

By the early '80s, I was the all-around media and graphics department. I was designing tour logos, program books, and album covers, and producing documentaries for John's nonprofit Windstar Foundation. John's departure from the management of Jerry Weintraub further opened a lot of creative doors for me, as his absence suddenly created a promotional and marketing vacuum.

John's new management, a hastily formed partnership of two of John's associates, Barney Wyckoff and Don Coder, started funneling more marketing jobs to me, so I was also now responsible for obtaining radio and television ads for local concert promoters, as well as distribution of print media and ad slicks. Nothing really qualified me for any of this, except I was now seen as a creative guy in the organization, the guy that would always say yes and figure it out later.

And that's how I also came to produce music videos. As producer of documentary films for the Windstar Foundation and producer of short background videos for concerts, I was the natural choice in the organization to produce this new medium of song promotion in the '80s for John.

In August 1981, MTV was launched and changed the way the recording industry promoted its artists and their products. Virtually overnight, the world of music moved from a predominately audio experience to a visual experience. AM radio, once the source of most people's introduction to a new recording, was now nearly obsolete, except for listening in the car. Even then, FM radio was more popular. For the recording companies, this development was a double-edged sword. It was positive because it introduced a whole new marketing channel. It was negative because not all artists were particularly appealing visually. Suddenly having a great voice or being a great musician became secondary to whatever visual stimulation you could invent.

The medium was not entirely new. In a sense, it was what I had been doing with the background concert visuals for years. Several earlier concepts for music video–based television programming had been around since the early 1960s. The Beatles had used music videos to promote their records and get their music on television without having to show up in person in the TV studio. The creative use of music videos within their 1964 film *A Hard Day's Night* (particularly the performance of the song "Can't Buy Me Love") led MTV to later honor the film's director, Richard Lester, with an award for basically inventing the music video. Many of us who had been producing short films, whose narrative was the lyrics of a song, had been strongly influenced by these early English videos shown on American television. The first truly visual band in America was the Monkees, whose television show was even more important than their radio play. Much of their content in the show was dedicated to what would later be called music videos—and that was a full fifteen years before MTV.

It's interesting to note that John's earliest background music video was "Mother Nature's Son," a Beatles song. The clip was produced in 1972 and was pretty basic stuff with John running down a mountain and through the woods being the nature guy he was.

By 1981, John's major string of hits had been over for a few years, and rock and pop artists dominated the MTV scene anyway. His record label, RCA Records, was losing interest in him by then, and he had a hard enough time getting them to promote his albums, let alone provide funds for music video production.

By the late '80s, everyone was producing content for music videos. More musical options were now cropping up. VH1 had a more diverse mix of artists presenting their videos, while MTV continued to feature rock and pop.

The first video I made for John that wasn't designed to be used as a visual backdrop in concerts was a Jimmy Webb song written for John titled "Postcard from Paris (Wish You Were Here)." When we originally began conceptualizing the idea, John wanted it to follow the song's narrative of a man traveling overseas, longing for his girl. But as the time got closer to begin shooting, his vision began to shift. We were scheduled to fly to Rome and shoot some of the outdoor scenes there among the landmarks mentioned in the song's lyrics. But John got skittish about traveling overseas as the prospect of a Gulf War was looking likely. I decided that I needed to shoot him singing the song in a studio, so I had at least a visual backbone to whatever else we agreed to do. John would fly into Orange County, where I lived, we'd shoot the live singing of the song at a studio in Mission Viejo, and then he'd fly back to Aspen the next day. He figured while we were together, we'd work out what we could do for the rest of the video and then schedule its shooting when he could find the time. This may seem a bit haphazard, but a great deal of decisions John made became real through this kind of on-the-fly thinking.

I picked him up at John Wayne Airport and set him up in a suite at the Ritz-Carlton at Monarch Beach. He didn't want to rent a car, so I said good-bye and made arrangements to pick him up in the morning for our shoot at noon. At about 8 a.m., I got a call from John. He had an idea and wanted me to come down earlier to work it out. I showed up at about 10 a.m.

The idea was to make the video more topical. We were sending men and machines into the Middle East, and it looked like the action required to free Kuwait was going to be a substantial war. Why not make our man in the song a soldier and the woman in the song the girl traveling through Europe? I would frame the song as a letter from home. I liked the idea and knew it would get more airplay because of its relevance to the news of the day.

The best part for John was that after he shot the live singing in the studio that day, he'd be done. The rest was up to me to finish. We decided that his wife at that time, Cassandra, would play the girl and that I could film her part when he returned to LA with her in a couple weeks. So that's what we did.

We shot him singing the song a few times, and I shot him in various positions writing the letter mentioned in the song, which we would later layer and edit over additional images. The shoot went without incident. Our videographer was George Adams, who John knew from other shoots I'd done and who was also with us on our Africa trip. It was always important to make John feel comfortable and secure in what was going on. John typically asked a lot of questions when we shot to make sure we were on the same page. By this shoot I had his complete confidence.

John with his Dobro guitar. Photo courtesy Lowell Norman.

We were finished by 4 p.m., and I had him back to his hotel by 5 p.m. He asked me to stick around a while, and we ended up going to dinner in Dana Point. This was an interesting time in John's life. He was still married to Cassandra, and his daughter Jesse Belle had just been born the year before.

The relationship with Cassandra was beginning to crumble, and the conversation that evening was dominated by this. As a friend, this news sounded alarm bells. I remembered how his breakup with Annie a decade earlier threw him for a loop. I could hear the pain in his voice, and it didn't sit well with me. Being the driver, I kept the alcohol to one drink. Not the same for John. We had a spirited conversation that ranged from soup to nuts regarding religion, God, and politics, and, of course, relationships. There's something about alcohol and deep conversations that allows you to open up, which John certainly did.

Over the years, we had several conversations about faith and family, relationships and kids, but this night all the stops were off. We left with a much deeper understanding of each other, which served as a reference point for our professional relationship in his final years.

The next morning, I drove over to pick him up and take him back to the airport where the Learjet was waiting. I don't think he had slept a wink, and I was hoping he wasn't going to try to sit in the pilot's seat on the way home. Sleep-deprived or not, he was in remarkably good spirits, which told me he was satisfied with the work we had done. Thankfully, I saw him climb into the jump seat, between the two pilots, for the ride back home.

Over the last seven years of his life, we produced several music videos, including "A Country Girl in Paris," "Flying for Me," "Potter's Wheel," "Let Us Begin (What Are We Making Weapons For?)" and "Don't Close Your Eyes, Tonight," among others. It was great having procured the skill necessary for the execution of these music videos in addition to my photography, but in truth, the secret was always in having the access.

John on the set in the Hollywood Hills to shoot a public service announcement about recycling.
John was years ahead of the crowd on the idea. Photo courtesy Lowell Norman.

Chapter 4

JOHNNY APPLESEED

In the years since John's passing, I have noticed attitudes both catching up to and falling behind his vision regarding the preservation of the natural world around us. Awareness has increased, but our treatment of the planet has not kept pace. I believe John and his message are exactly what is missing in the planetary discussion of the twenty-first century. He was smart, articulate, and undeniably likable when discussing protecting and saving the planet. He had a way of making the message palatable for everyone.

Without being judgmental about it or overly strident in any way, he opened our eyes and minds to the nature we could lose. By celebrating it through his music, he laid the groundwork for our understanding of the acute need to be more diligent about maintaining a healthy environment. And he put it in songs we could all sing. His nonconfrontational approach was by design. Through it he was able to communicate the importance of nature without drawing lines in the sand, without polarizing left or right. He merely pointed it out. And, like John Muir a century before him, he practiced a sort of soft touch, a reverence when dealing with or communicating the issues of the environment. Like Emerson and Thoreau, he articulated a respect for the wild and our place in it through his poetry of song. Like Johnny Appleseed, he simply just planted the seed.

Today, the environmental movement has become largely misanthropic, cultivating a view of humanity as something entirely negative, a plague to be eradicated. John, on the other hand, saw as much in humanity as he did in nature, and he knew the source of the environment's healing was going to be man's ingenuity, vision, and resourcefulness. He expressed it in song as possibility and opportunity. And it's why he created the Windstar Foundation—to foster humanity's inventiveness and to create a supportive platform from which change could be demonstrated.

He picked as his cofounder a man rooted in conflict resolution, educator and lecturer Tom Crum. Like John, Tom was nonconfrontational, and this approach—this open, nonpolarizing stance—was to be the cornerstone of Windstar philosophy. The idea that all positions and all opinions have equal weight was critical to the mission of Windstar, which set out to solve some of the most perplexing issues in the world, including hunger, disease, and conflict. Windstar was founded in 1976 by John and Tom with the mission to "educate, inspire, and empower children and adults to create responsible choice through community and global action for a healthy and sustainable environment." The physical domain of the foundation was 957 acres near Snowmass, Colorado, a short drive down-valley from Aspen. But, as John said many times, Windstar was not him or a location but "a place inside you." He wanted Windstar to be in the heart so it would forever influence how we live.

You could say Windstar was indeed in the heart of John from an early age. Growing up US Air Force brat, moving from state to state, and having a difficult time both making friends and keeping them, he turned to the most comfortable place he knew: his love of nature. It was a friend he could take with him from place to place. While other kids were playing cowboys and Indians, his sensitivity tended to side with the Indians—and, more specifically, how they managed to live in harmony with nature. His fascination was not in their bows and arrows but in the gentle way he saw them live their lives. His bicycle was his pony, and his playground was often the most challenging tree he could climb. He'd spend hours climbing trees and gazing outward from his perch, pretending clouds were smoke signals. I think he deeply respected the strong family structure of our Native Americans. The idea of living off the land, together in a village of tents, appealed to his vision of community, harmony, and permanence—the very things he missed the most in his itinerant life.

As he matured, so did these childhood ideals, but they never disappeared. Windstar was, in the simplest of terms, a sanctuary for John, a community of like-minded men and women who all shared a vision of true community, a place of both abundance and sustainability.

John's big-picture view of our planet and its preservation was consistent in everything he did. It was in his live performances. It was in his work with The Hunger Project. It was in his work with the Windstar Foundation. It was the focus of every film project we worked on together. It was the backdrop for most of the still photography and music videos I did with him. It was in his interviews. And, above all else, it was in his songs.

My introduction to John in my early twenties coincided with my own interest in backpacking. I was already going on trips up in the mountains to some of my favorite places in the Sierras, so it was fortuitous for me to get to work with him. I looked and dressed like the guy on the cover of that *Rocky Mountain High* album. I felt a kindred spirit there.

John's music was the soundtrack for such activity. What surf and beach parties were to the Beach Boys, the mountains were to John Denver. My first touring dates with John were often at colleges and universities, and in those early years—1973 and 1974—our audiences were predominantly college students and young adults, nature-loving people like me. Culturally and musically, young society had just evolved from a hippie thing to a nature thing. John fit perfectly into that, and into the me generation of introspection through Eastern philosophies and self-improvement seminars like est (Erhard Seminars Training). It was an interesting mix, and he became something of a leader in this movement, whether he saw himself that way or not. When you think about John, you think mountains or nature. It was by design, but it was also real, which is why it worked.

In fact, once I got to know John, I realized that it was *exactly* who he was. He wasn't a fancy guy. He liked kicking around in the mountains, and he liked camping, backpacking, and living as much off the land as was practical. *Nature.* That was his thing. It wasn't a gimmick. He lived it.

Later, when he started turning up on television in comedy sketches and in dance numbers that distracted (if briefly, but on the grandest of scales) from making music, I personally think some of this younger core audience went elsewhere. To many he had lost connection to his overarching life's work. Although he opened the door to an older and arguably more affluent market, his base started to collapse, and he created a credibility gap with many of his early fans. They wondered where their nature-loving country boy had gone, maybe even thinking he had sold out.

But John never lost touch with that side, even if it got eclipsed by the TV lights for a time. In the first month I worked with him, we traveled on tour through the Southwest. When we got to Tucson, we went up Mount Lemmon (at over 9,000 feet, it's the highest point in the Santa Catalina Mountains), and I took my first photos of him. I believe there were just four of us: John, Kris O'Connor, John Sommers, and me. We also drove around Tucson in a rented station wagon, as we did in a lot of cities, and we saw the house where he'd lived as a kid. (Since he was the son of a US Army Air Corps pilot, John lived in a lot of places growing up.) We went by a Presbyterian church, where John said he'd first met God. We explored a lot on the road in those earlier days, often retracing the rural playgrounds of his youth. Early on I got the sense that his childhood had been a lonely one, and perhaps it was then that nature and the environments around him became his friends. I was always struck by how it was always the places he remembered so vividly, rather than the people who lived there.

We spent a lot of time in the Rocky Mountains shooting film for the live shows, a lot of which was for all five movements of his "Season Suite." One day, John drove me about an hour outside of Aspen to the site of a dam project, and the mountain was being torn apart for it. This was quite upsetting to John. We shot film to coincide with the line, "While they try to tear the mountains down to bring in a couple more / More people, more scars upon the land," from "Rocky Mountain High." Although it was pretty graphic, we ultimately didn't use it. It was too confrontational, too polarizing for John's taste. He found the negative images of humanity's "scars upon the land" to be less compelling than wild nature—another hint of the subtlety of his message, and how he envisioned his film content to communicate. "Don't alienate, stay open to all points of view—even those you cannot embrace." That was the Windstar way.

John was deeply angry about what he viewed as humanity's overstepping, but he didn't express it with outbursts. He was realistic about the changing world in which we lived, and he just acknowledged it with a serious determination to alter the direction the best he could. His outlook was straightforward and matter-of-fact, and his warning was, "This is the way the world is headed. We need to do what we can to manage it." He responded to his own anger with action.

He often talked about his celebrity and the responsibility he felt that came with it. He was always amazed by the influence he had, and, accordingly, he didn't take it for granted. He wanted to use it toward worthwhile ends. As I found out when I directed the film *I Want to Live,* which was about bringing attention to the plight of hunger worldwide, and which we took to calling the "hunger documentary," we had total access to Washington, D.C., and all the political opportunities there. From 1977 until we completed shooting in 1979, we could go anywhere and were welcomed everywhere. I had an open permit to film anywhere in D.C. I could set interview dates with any senator or representative, and instead of getting the usual "We'll get back to you" response, they all made themselves available without hesitation.

After all, John Denver was a popular guy, owning a broad audience base. They knew that any association with him only expanded their constituencies. My coproducer and writer, Keith Blume, and I interviewed notable political figures such as Vice President Walter Mondale, Hubert Humphrey, and Lillian Carter, along with a dozen others for the hunger documentary, and John wasn't even there! He didn't need to be; they all knew we were from John's organization and took it as an honor to appear in John's film. That was the kind of respect he was universally given.

I went with John to D.C., where he would often testify at hearings, which were usually fact-finding inquiries. John was a perfect representative. He spoke skillfully on why we shouldn't be drilling for oil in Alaska, why ending hunger was an idea whose time had come, why initiating a civilians-in-space policy might garner more support for NASA, why censoring music was a bad idea, and why opening cultural ties to the Soviet Union might actually bring our nations closer. John was also a confident speaker on such things; he never went into anything unprepared. And if he ever experienced apprehension about anything, you wouldn't have known it. He was the epitome of self-confidence and control during those times.

This was at a time when my particular focus within Windstar was working on the hunger documentary, but John always had multiple projects on his plate, and he was dedicating a lot of time to the preservation of Alaska. I admit, it sometimes annoyed me that he was distracted by so many projects going at the same time.

Windstar produced four versions of the hunger documentary over a period of three years, partly because John kept finding more people to interview. More voices to join his. Eventually he said, "We're through, print it." A year and a half later, the Carter administration was gone and much of the film had become obsolete by virtue of the new Reagan administration, with a new focus and agenda. I got to work on some of his other projects, too, but I wanted the emphasis to be on eradicating hunger, which I saw as the largest and most acute issue with which we were involved.

Others in the organization (especially musicians and those whose jobs were specific to touring) were somewhat threatened by all of John's activism. They saw it as a distraction from the music and the live performances. A common complaint I heard regularly and frequently from the band was that John needed to be focusing on music instead of flying everywhere and trying to save the world. In some ways they were right; John was able to pursue his passion projects because of who he was, a musician and public figure. He was John Denver, writer and singer of songs, many of which were about these larger issues facing us all.

Songwriting and performing is what he did best, and with the benefit of hindsight, it is what will endure as his most visible cultural contribution. But I also like to believe that there has been a ripple effect from the work we did on all the planetary issues, hunger included. Others have carried the torch and made worthy and incrementally successful efforts at saving our world. I think John would see both things if he were here: that good work has been done, and that it isn't even close to enough.

The time John spent in Alaska led to a three-hour filmed documentary produced by ABC. For many, it was their first in-depth look at both the challenges and opportunities Alaska offered. I wasn't on that trip, but I did repurpose some of the footage that had been shot into two music videos of John's Alaska-oriented songs "To the Wild Country" and "American Child."

I once made a film for the Department of Energy (a new governmental agency at the time under the Carter administration) on passive solar energy. I started the project at Mesa Verde National Park in southwestern Colorado, a perfect example of passive solar energy. It had been constructed with the heat and light of the sun's energy in mind, the dwellings even being positioned in the best way for the sun to generate passive power. Mesa Verde is dug out on the side of a hill and was a city for nomadic Paleo-Indians dating back thousands of years. It's an excellent documentation of life on the North American continent long before the existence of the United States.

I had to take out a $2 million damage policy for the single day we shot film at Mesa Verde, in case we trashed the place. They didn't know the respect and reverence John held for such national treasures. The cliff-dwelling part of the park was closed to tourists for that one day so we could shoot, and it was a magnificent experience. We had Mesa Verde all to ourselves, save for the park ranger, who always kept us in sight. John had a blast crawling around the cliff dwellings, perhaps recapturing some of his boyhood fantasies.

The film was called *Sun-up, A Passive Approach*, and it was the story of the building of a passive solar dormitory at Colorado Rocky Mountain School. A working experiment and ongoing research laboratory, the dorm used no outside electricity whatsoever. Designed by passive solar pioneer Ron Shore (who had helped design the passive solar elements in John's home), its heating and cooling, lighting, and electrical needs were all handled by passive solar- and wind-powered generators. It was state of the art for the time—or was it? Places had been built with the sun in mind for thousands of years, as Mesa Verde itself had demonstrated. We had only gotten away from it with the advent of our nation's power grid over the last hundred years or so.

John was the host and narrator of the film, explaining what passive energy was. It took a year and a half for the whole film to come together, as I needed to document the construction of the dormitory from the day they broke ground right up until the day students moved in.

These and other Windstar film projects (some airing on television, others for specific audiences) were every bit as important to John as his music. After all, it was all the same story, all part of his lifelong narrative.

We all know "Rocky Mountain High" and "Sunshine on My Shoulders," but there were other songs, sometimes entire albums, with a purposeful theme of making the world a better place. One of his lesser-known albums from 1986 called *One World* is a great example of this. The record included songs like the title track, "Flying for Me," and one called "Let Us Begin (What Are We Making Weapons For?)" as John incorporated nuclear proliferation into his message of global preservation. By now it was impossible to separate the music, the man, and what Windstar stood for. It was all part of the same mission.

Inspired by his time with Jacques Cousteau, John wrote "Calypso," a huge hit for him in the '70s. All proceeds from the song, which were substantial, went to the Cousteau Society. Photo courtesy John Denver photo archive.

Chapter 5

SWIMMING WITH WHALES

Humpback whales travel from Hawaii, where they live during the winter months, to Alaska, which is their summer home. They make this annual 6,000-mile round trip riding a liquid highway of currents and ocean temperatures. Schools of humpbacks may be found fairly close to shore along the Kona coast each winter. They are particularly active and playful, as we all are, when visiting Hawaii. But it's not exactly vacation that brings the whales south. Humpbacks feed on the abundant plankton in the waters around the Big Island of Hawaii, and the warmer waters are where they prefer to birth their young.

In the mid-1970s, whales were quite the hip creatures. Many species had been hunted to near extinction, and the humpbacks were headed in that same direction. So, they became a cause célèbre for a generation of young people who just a few years earlier had been protesting the war in Vietnam and were now searching for other injustices to correct.

John Denver was certainly part of that culture. He famously embraced nature and all that was threatening her in his many hit records. With "Calypso," he sang a song of celebration for Captain Jacques Cousteau and those who tirelessly explored the oceans and fought for the creatures in them. It was John's experience and the friendship he forged with Cousteau that moved him to feature the plight of the humpback in one of his annual television specials.

I received a call from John on an early weekday afternoon in the fall of 1978. He was in Los Angeles working on his newest television special, and he had an idea for a segment. What was I doing the following week? Well, it wouldn't have mattered what I was doing. I worked for him, and literally on the spur of the moment, he'd decided that he was going to go to Hawaii to swim with the humpbacks. John, who was usually a fairly well-grounded guy, got these fits of fancy once in a while—dreams, impulsive and not— that most of us think about and then let go. But because he had the means, motive, and energy to turn these seemingly crazy ideas into reality, he acted on his impulses often without regard for logistical challenges. Dealing with all that was someone else's job. The challenges for this adventure would be significant, and given the time constraints, maybe even impossible.

Impossibility never prevented John Denver from doing exactly what he wanted to do. He was equal parts excitable kid and serious-minded artist in his quest to capture and celebrate the natural world around him.

Here was the plan: We were to take a crew to the Big Island of Hawaii and get footage of John in the water swimming with the whales off the Kona coast. Sounds simple enough, right? It was not.

Two elements in this plan raised immediate red flags. Number one was safety. Jumping into the ocean with the largest of earth's mammals has its unknowns. Keeping John safe in the water, along with a crew outfitted in scuba gear and large cameras requiring protection from the water, is one thing; add a thirty-ton sea creature into the mix and you've got a potential disaster. Number two was filming. When shooting film from the boat, we sought to capture John jumping into whale-infested waters . . . but we had no idea what we'd see. We'd need angles, and lots of perspective (meaning lots of cameras positioned to maximize our field of view), when this blessed event happened. And chances were that we would get only one shot at it, if any.

So now we were talking about way more assets than a couple of guys on a boat documenting a singer swimming with a whale. We were talking multiple boats, several camera operators shooting at various angles, an airplane or helicopter circling above with more cameras (including a high-speed motion-picture camera), a crew of about twenty, a broadcast-quality video camera in a watertight casing with an umbilical cord to a recorder on the boat—all of which, by the way, had never been done before. We also required a separate crew for maintaining all the scuba gear, a safety control expert to shadow John's every move, and a couple of PhD oceanographers who specialize in the behavior of humpback whales—need I go on?

Also, what made John think the whales were going to *want* to swim with him? They might just totally shine him on, dive too deep to film, swim away, or—horror of horrors—smack him with a tail, leaving him injured or worse. There was a certain arrogance in this adventure that only those of us who were not consumed by his whale passion understood. To me, the risk-to-reward ratio seemed tilted the wrong way. Still, I wasn't really risking anything (meaning *my* life and *my* safety) and it would be quite an adventure, so I was happy to play along. Because it was a location shoot for network television, John would have to use the network's production staff for all the principal video footage. He wanted me flying overhead shooting stills and motion-picture film.

To me, this was the best possible gig on this shoot, up and away from all the challenges and confines facing the water-based crew. My ride was a single-engine Citaborea (*Citaborea* is *aerobatic* spelled backward and the common nickname for the American Champion 7-GCAA). It's built for turns and tricks in the sky. The two-seater plane looked like a Piper Cub. It had a narrow fuselage with a high wing and tandem seating, which made it a good shooting platform, as long as you didn't mind hanging out of one of the side doors. I sat in front with four cameras in my lap, including a CinePro 16mm high-speed motion-picture camera weighing about thirty pounds. The CinePro shoots at two hundred frames per second, or about ten times faster than normal speed. It allows for much more detail and slows the motion to diminish vibration and shaky camera movements. Which was fortunate because the flying was bumpy. Not so much because of the instability of the air, but rather because of the constant turning of our plane to allow us the best shooting angle.

I loved every minute of it. My pilot was a young guy named Mike. He began his flight training as a youth and played football for Ohio State. He was a big guy, almost as tall as my six-foot six-inch frame but much wider. Mike worried about our weight for the plane, because together we pulled about 420 pounds, plus my equipment. Luckily it never was an issue, although I think he adjusted and hedged his bets by not fully fueling the plane every day. We were about the same age—he was twenty-eight and waiting for a full-time gig with one of the airlines.

Every day of the shoot, we arrived early at the airport located high on a mountain above the Kona coast. He would check out the plane and I would load it with all our supplies, which also included food and drink because we spent the day—all day—in the air with only one brief bathroom and fuel stop.

The weather was perfect all week. The skies were smooth for flying, the ocean calm. Now if only the whales would cooperate, we'd be all set.

The water crew was divided among three boats. One was the *Ailhenuee*, a sixty-foot sailing catamaran. The two other boats were Zodiacs. The *Ailhenuee* was the mother ship, and from there the crew would race to the whales in the Zodiacs. The first few days were uneventful, except for the fact that one of the scuba divers somehow screwed up John's scuba tank and John almost drowned. Coordinating all the efforts was a big task and it took a while to get our operation running smoothly. We were a long way from functioning like Navy SEALs, that's for sure.

After a couple of days watching the whales seemingly laugh at us as we chased them just beyond our reach, John came up with the brilliant idea of just floating out and letting them come to us. This turned what would have been a wasted week into an eventful one. Humpbacks are known as gentle giants. They actually seem interested in humans and perform for an audience by swimming and playing when boats are near. From the air, the water was clear enough to see the whales underwater, their silhouettes dwarfing the smaller boats. Several times, when the whales would come alongside the boats, we saw John attempt to make contact. He would jump in with his tank on, and so would the videographer with all his underwater gear. The whales would gently say no thanks, and off they'd go.

Understand that every hour we spent in Hawaii cost a lot of money. The exact value of what we might get for all our effort began to weigh on John, who was acting as both producer and director. During the first two days of our adventure, John was laser-focused on the whales and his earnest quest to interact with them. By the third day, having had no real luck, he started to question the validity of his original idea.

John began to consider that maybe the segment should simply be about hanging out with the whales, and his perspective on seeing them up close. Perhaps we could use the video as a backdrop for a song performance. We discussed different approaches. I told him I thought I'd gotten some interesting footage, even though it wasn't of him swimming with the whales. At least it could be used in a documentary.

Of course, as this was 1978, long before the digital era of photography, we wouldn't know what we actually had until we developed the film. Same with the 16mm film. But all things being equal, I was confident I was getting good footage, and if the camera was functioning as it should, I was okay. This was an example of having everything in place for perfect execution but lacking access.

As for the video guys, they had really gotten precious little usable underwater footage. Constrained in those early years of video technology by the need for bright light and that damn umbilical cord that tied the camera to the video recorder on deck, they already had two strikes against them before they even entered the water.

John decided to give it one more day. If it happened that we got into a position that allowed him to jump in the water with the whales, then we just might get the footage we'd hoped for. If not, we would edit together what we did have and maybe get an E for effort.

The whales must have been listening. Our last day of shooting was a Saturday. Once again, I was flying overhead only 100 to 150 feet above the Kona coast. Back and forth, circling around, spotting the whales, sending down the coordinates to the *Ailhenuee*, and then circling until the boats arrived. This was our routine, and now, on our fifth day, we had it down to a science. If only something magical would happen.

Midafternoon, after a morning of spotting and jockeying for position to get ahead of where the whales were heading, our three boats stopped and waited. John, having abandoned his quest to swim with the mammals, had taken off his scuba gear. The videographer jumped in with his camera and took up a position between the two hulls of the catamaran, where he hoped to catch something on camera to justify all our efforts. The whales crept slowly into view. Soon they were all around the *Ailhenuee*. They comprised a whole pod of whales. Mothers and their calves, old barnacled whales blowing air out of their blowholes, breaching underwater and slapping their tails on the water's surface.

This is what we had hoped for the entire time. Mike swung the plane around into perfect position over the action and tilted my side to the sea, so I had a perfect vantage point for shooting, and just as I pulled the trigger and the film began to whir, John jumped into the water with only a face mask and snorkel and swam alongside a whale. The whale turned and seemed to acknowledge his presence and allowed John to hang out with him for a couple of minutes. It wouldn't surprise me if John had started singing to the whale in a gesture of friendship, and for all I know, he did. Whales sing too, you know.

I shot until the film load ended, then I grabbed my Nikon and shot stills until that load was exhausted, and then, ninety seconds later, it was over. The whales swam out to sea.

Cruising overhead now at only eighty feet or so above the boats with the engine at idle for the moment, we could see and hear John and the crew shouting and jumping and high-fiving each other. Their exuberance was like the moment all the saucers left earth after making contact in the movie *Close Encounters of the Third Kind.*

Mike did his celebrating by climbing our airplane up a few hundred feet and doing a barrel roll.

What a charmed existence John Denver had. To summon the talents and skills of a couple dozen professionals, take them 3,000 miles, put them on boats and planes and hope to find and swim with whales, all on a few days' notice, with no preplanning or script notes, no trial and error, only what we found as we went . . . that was an adventure.

And, as it turned out, we were damn lucky to get what we did. The high-speed footage of John in the water with the whale, shot from about a hundred feet at two hundred frames a second, was the only usable action footage we got of that magical moment, as well as some still shots I took after the film ran out in the movie camera. John produced the segment for his television show anyway, using about one minute of the footage.

He would tell me later, "It was worth it." I'm not so sure. Looking back now, it seemed a pointless and somewhat arrogant exercise to me. I mean, really, was the plight of the humpback whales any more remedied by taking a swim with them on national TV? Considering the sizable risk of people and equipment, time and money, it seemed a very expensive exercise in futility, and, I might add, ego . . . but damn, it was a fun week!

John enjoying the front row center view of Victoria Falls, Zimbabwe, Africa. Photo courtesy Lowell Norman.

Chapter 6

ON THE FRONT LINES OF WORLD HUNGER

There's a bronze statue of John Denver at Red Rocks, the stunning outdoor amphitheater outside Denver, Colorado, where major musical acts have been performing for more than a century. The red rocks from which it took its name serve as dramatic barriers for the steep cliff onto which the outdoor theater was built. The Beatles played there in 1964 and Jimi Hendrix in 1968. U2's famous "Sunday Bloody Sunday" video was shot in performance there in 1983. And, between 1972 and 1989, John Denver played there seventeen times.

Spirit is the name of the grand statue, and it's appropriate that it is displayed at such an idyllic natural site as Red Rocks. (Red Rocks is also the home of the Colorado Music Hall of Fame, of which John was the first inductee.) John's guitar is draped over his shoulder as an eagle is perched on his arm.

But the original home of *Spirit* was another idyllic location: Snowmass, Colorado, where John had created the Windstar Foundation as an ambitious real-life version of his hopeful songs. Its first project was the preservation of the thousand acres of beautiful mountain scenery in Snowmass, where the organization itself would reside during its lifespan from 1976 to 2012. But its larger purpose was support toward causes like ending world hunger through self-sustaining agriculture and food production, along with other passive technologies. It would focus on renewable energy resources and self-sustaining food production.

Windstar would be John's songs in action, a vehicle to promote his passion for a healthy planet. It would be an educational starting point to encourage others. When President Kennedy ambitiously announced a determination to reach the moon by the end of the 1960s, his words became a self-fulfilling prophecy. He knew the technology of the day had rendered it possible. His ambition rendered it a reality. Windstar's concept was similar. The organization would support its causes through film and media production, interactive seminars, and a news and information magazine. An informed society could end world hunger and restore the planet collectively.

A year after the creation of Windstar, The Hunger Project was founded by Werner Erhard, John Denver, Bob Fuller, Joan Holmes, Dana Meadows, and Roy Prosterman. The common goal was to raise the awareness and political will of the American people so that worldwide hunger could be ended. At its core, at least in the minds of both John and Werner, and like Windstar, The Hunger Project was to be a demonstration platform, an opportunity to apply some of the principles Werner expounded in his seminars, which, by now, had gained national attention. World hunger was the perfect project to test the validity of these principles. If enough people could be convinced that world hunger could be eradicated by the year 2000, and worked toward that end, they would change the pervasive belief that hunger will always exist, as it is the inevitable result of poverty, overpopulation, and a host of other chronic problems of many developing nations. If you could mobilize the efforts of people dedicated to the challenge of ending hunger on the planet, imagine what other seemingly impossible obstacles we could conquer.

On a personal and professional level, the ambitious pursuits of these projects would expand my creative role within John's world. My film work to date had primarily been content for his live performances, but now, with the advent of Windstar, I became a documentary filmmaker.

One weekday afternoon in the spring of 1977, I got a phone call from John. He was in his Learjet flying from San Francisco back to Aspen. The call was muffled and he was breaking up in those pre–cell phone days, so he kept it short. He had just seen a film called *The Hungry Planet* and had met its producer, Keith Blume. He loved Keith's film, but he wanted me to view it and perhaps re-edit it to include current information. He was sending Keith down to see me, and together we would try to figure out what to do with it.

What he was really saying was that the film could be redone and customized for The Hunger Project. And by putting John Denver into the piece, it could be seen by a wider audience. For the next two years, I worked as director and coproducer (with Keith) on the one-hour documentary film titled *I Want to Live*. Its message was simple and profound, a mirror of one of John's nonprofit's missions: end worldwide hunger. With the political will, appropriate technology, and basic farming education and implementation, we as a global society can come together and end hunger as we know it. Ending hunger was an idea whose time had come. Its message is as relevant today as it was then, yet one that has proven stubborn to implement.

We pulled in other people and organizations in our effort to put a spotlight on hunger. Singer-songwriter Harry Chapin was a friend of ours, and he had his own project, World Hunger Year—a nonprofit that still exists, now under the name WhyHunger. Harry was a deeply passionate and charitable artist, donating proceeds from many of his gigs to such causes. He contributed his time and worked with us on the hunger film. His own great work was cut short just a few years later in 1981 when he died in a car crash.

John was at the height of his popularity at the time of this film, which, of course, had everything to do with its creation. If John Denver were part of such a project, we knew that it would be seen. And so it was. We sent the film everywhere. I remember sending it to the pope. I received a letter from the Vatican acknowledging receipt, but I don't know if the pope ever actually saw the film. John finally met Pope John Paul II some years later and he reportedly knew of John's involvement and activities regarding world hunger and other related human rights issues, so you never know.

The film would be shown to different groups and meetings as a backdrop to get the audience up to speed on the state of world hunger. It was distributed far and wide, and it proved effective to those who viewed it. Years after finishing the film, I was approached by a man who was president of a world relief organization who credited seeing our film as the catalyst of his involvement in world hunger. Quite an endorsement. You wonder sometimes if your efforts actually reach anyone, and then you hear testaments like that. Besides the private screenings, the film would also be shown on public television stations, and it can now be found on YouTube.

John was playing the big 15,000-seat halls at this time, and he would frequently host a press conference several hours ahead of a show. He was always pitching Windstar, the film, and the hunger issue in general, a topic on which he had growing knowledge. John was a great student, and he became well versed in everything he was involved in. He was always in 100 percent, and that included the fight against hunger. This made him an excellent and articulate public speaker. He never opened his mouth until he had done all the research and had something to say. And, as those of us who were to some degree responsible for content knew, it had to be accurate.

Then, during the actual concert, he would perform the song "I Want to Live" after speaking about hunger. We usually did not show the short music video I had made for the song on the screen behind him during those shows, but I remember John wanting to spring it on a Harrah's Lake Tahoe audience who had just been eating dinner before John performed. John's manager, Jerry Weintraub, was hesitant and said to me, "You're not gonna show this to all these people eating dinner, are you?" I said, "Yeah, that's what John wants me to do." He said, "Hell no! We're not going to do that." Jerry then wisely dissuaded John from displaying the video that included graphic images of the effects of hunger. People were coming to be uplifted by a John Denver concert, not plunged into depression. John came to his senses, relented, and I never showed the short film to a live audience. But he still managed to incorporate its message into the show by performing the song.

In 1978, President Jimmy Carter wrote Executive Order 12078 to form the Presidential Commission on World Hunger. John Denver was asked to be on the commission, and it was at about the same time we had begun shooting the *I Want to Live* documentary.

I was at the first meeting of the commission at the White House with my film crew. John's involvement on the commission and subsequent friendship with President Carter opened virtually every door for us, so Keith and I took full advantage, interviewing many of the political leaders of that day. John was the biggest-selling recording artist in the world at that time, and political figures were only too happy to have an association with his celebrity.

John wasn't doing this work for recognition; in fact, he was using his worldwide popularity to further a cause close to his heart. At the same time, it stung when, given his fame and credentials, John wasn't invited to take part in the "We Are the World" project. There was not a more qualified singer (or public figure of any type, for that matter) to sing and speak passionately about the state of hunger on our planet. Beyond that, John's extraordinary singing voice was more inherently sincere and emotional than many of those included. He had been singing about the world and its issues his whole life. But instead, there was Dan Aykroyd and La Toya Jackson up there singing with all the popular musicians of the time. The other perplexing thing about his being left off the invitation list was how close his manager, Jerry Weintraub, was to the project's creator, entertainment manager Ken Kragen. They were friends. Ken's office was just down the hall from Jerry's, and Ken had intimate knowledge of John's activism. Ken's later explanation of John's exclusion had to do with his vision of who qualified as a participant. In his vision the song and accompanying video was to be *rock's* response to the crisis in Africa, and in no way did John fit into the rock category. A lame explanation, to be kind.

Although hurt, John never complained about his exclusion and simply stayed on his own path, just as he had always done with his music. It was just as well. Jerry Weintraub and John both always seemed more interested in keeping John Denver projects independent from other such collaborative ventures anyway, and perhaps Jerry felt that he didn't want his boy mixed in the clutter of all these lesser artists. We'll never know the exact reason, but one thing is clear: Given John's exemplary qualifications as an articulate spokesperson, this was a snub.

The production of the *I Want to Live* series (four versions of the same film) was really just the beginning of this type of work for me. Five years later, I was asked if I would consider producing another documentary on world hunger, this time for The Hunger Project. It would entail documenting a fact-finding trip to Africa with John.

I wanted to do it, but there was now family to consider. My son Tyler was just three months old, and I hated to leave him and my wife at that time. But Deb agreed that it would be a great opportunity and encouraged me to seize it. I organized my film crew, packed my bags, and joined John and the others in Paris.

But on the flight from LA to Paris, I began to feel sick. It was a feeling I had experienced many times before: I was trying to pass a kidney stone. I knew how difficult a kidney stone could be, and I didn't like the idea of fighting one in a developing nation where medical help was hard to find. After arriving in Paris and conferring with John and the president of The Hunger Project, Joan Holmes, I got back on a plane for home with the promise of catching up with them in Somalia four days later, if I could manage to pass the stone.

In the meantime, my videographer, George Adams, would act as director. George had at least as much experience directing as I had, but John much preferred working with people in his inner circle. Otherwise, he could be difficult. George was not really in the family, so I kept my fingers crossed that they would work well together. Fortunately, the first few days were in Burkina Faso, a small country in sub-Saharan Africa that John needed to visit for his duties as ambassador with UNICEF (United Nations International Children's Emergency Fund). There would be no need for shooting much film during that part of the trip anyway, except to obtain some B-roll footage. As I flew back home, I began feeling better, and by the time I landed, I had either passed the stone or it had passed further along its route out and was no longer causing me pain. My urologist took X-rays the next day and found no reason I shouldn't continue my trip. A day later, with pain meds in my bag, I was flying back to join John and my crew.

I've often thought that my pain at the beginning of this adventure was somehow connected to my apprehension of witnessing the pain of children I was sure to encounter. My pain was a problem of the privileged as I headed to document the very real problems of hunger on the African continent. In fact, *problem* seems an insufficient word to use for this largest of human topics.

And I would be heading to the hungriest pockets of the world. I did my best to prepare to witness the most desperate of situations. My own first child, Grant, had died as an infant after open-heart surgery, and that experience—the worst of my life—was also fresh in my mind. I didn't cherish the thought of watching the pain of mothers cradling their suffering children.

On top of that, I would soon learn I was effectively heading into a war zone. There were guns of warring tribes everywhere in Somalia. For security reasons, John would end up spending more time in his hotel room than in the thick of things because of his very public role as both entertainment icon and hunger ambassador.

The trip proved to be monumental in my life, and I took the time to document the events of those days. What follows here comes from memory bolstered by my daily notes of the events of this extraordinary trip. It's the story of a pop music crew member venturing into the world of global political crises, beginning with an introduction of all the players on our African journey. Here's who was on the trip:

John Denver: Host and reporter for the documentary

Joan Holmes: President of The Hunger Project and coproducer

Lowell Norman (myself): Director and coproducer

George Adams: Videographer

Jim Jack: Grip, video technician and sound recorder

Werner Krutein: Grip and photographer

Ted Long: Assistant to Joan Holmes

Jon Duell: Research and copywriting

Martin Luther King III: Observer (Martin really was an observer with no official involvement with production, and yes, he's the son of Martin Luther King Jr.)

We also had a Swiss pilot and copilot of our chartered Falcon 55 and a few others we met along the way who helped us navigate through the sometimes hostile procedural and political obstacles we encountered.

My layover was in Rome, before flying to Somalia via Ethiopia and Saudi Arabia. The flight was arduous. I brought with me extra videotape, another Ikegami camera, and a bunch of documents The Hunger Project asked me to take over. My newborn son, Tyler, was so cute that I could barely stand leaving again. He was laughing and had grown out of his stomach issues, thank God. I missed him and Deb already.

After landing in Rome, it took me three hours to get the equipment and myself to the hotel. I worried about how I was going to handle it all when I arrived at the Somalia airport. Plus, I wasn't even sure my flight arrival time in Somalia would match arrangements to be picked up. There would be no way of contacting the crew, so I just had to have faith it would work out and decided to make the most of my half day off in Rome with a taxi ride through the city the next morning. When I opened my suitcase, I found Deb had slipped in a card and an audio cassette of Tyler playing while she gave him a bath. So cute. I listened to it on my Walkman as I went to sleep.

I woke up late the next morning, so Rome would have to wait. No time to sightsee. On the recommendation of the hotel concierge, I left for the airport several hours before my flight. It turned out to be great advice. The Rome airport was nuts, and getting through customs was crazy. Next to my departure line at the Rome airport was a roped-off area being demolished. It was where terrorists had placed a bomb and killed several people a few weeks prior. A reminder perhaps of the uncertainty I could encounter in this part of the world as I traveled alone. I just prayed that someone was waiting in Somalia for me.

Once on the plane, I found I was literally the only passenger flying first class. It felt very weird. The back of the plane was packed with Arabs and Somalis heading home. Some of the Somalis looked so poor I wondered what brought them to Rome, of all places, and how they managed the fare. I got a meal on the first leg of the flight to Jeddah, Saudi Arabia. I don't think anyone else did. I must've looked like a real ugly American riding in first class eating a meal with actual silverware and a cloth napkin all alone, with everyone else packed in the back like sardines. I had a thought that I was going to feel the guilt of my privilege many times on this trip.

I first landed in Jeddah, a Saudi coastal city on the Red Sea. The plane parked quite a way from the terminal, and three-fourths of the plane's passengers got off. I couldn't because I was told it was not advisable. We sat there another hour out on the hot tarmac with the plane doors open. Most of the crew had left the plane, and the stairs that allowed the passengers to exit the plane had now been pushed away. I wondered, *was this to keep us on or to keep unwanted visitors off?* They bused the passengers to the terminal that looked to be about a quarter mile away. It was a little unsettling with no crew, except for one flight attendant, and no way off.

Eventually a fresh crew arrived, and we took off. An hour or so later, we arrived in Addis Ababa, Ethiopia. Same deal. Leaving the plane was not allowed. No one got on the plane in Saudi Arabia, and no one got on the plane in Ethiopia. I got the feeling Somalia was the end of the world and no one wanted to go there. I was still all alone in first class. I got to know my flight attendant. After all, I was her only customer on this flight, and although her English was not great, I had managed to pick up a little info on what I might expect when landing at our last stop: Mogadishu, Somalia. "Where do you and the pilots stay when there?" I asked the flight attendant. "Oh, we never stay in Mogadishu," she said. "It's not safe!"

The runway there was shorter than most, so the plane had to touch down early so it could use the whole runway to land. Passengers disembarked and then waited alongside the airplane for their luggage. They had luggage carts, and then you pushed the carts over the tarmac to customs. Once through customs, you exited the terminal to the street where someone would be waiting for you. Sounded simple enough.

We landed and the procedure began, just as I was told. The first thing I noticed as I exited the plane in Mogadishu were the two wrecked airline planes that had been shoved off the runway like broken toys. This airport was the final, deadly site of one of the most famous terrorist skyjackings in history, and one of those planes was still sitting next to the runway, rusting away.

The other plane looked like it was just abandoned and left to bake in the Somalia sun. Although I was the only white person in sight, for once I wasn't the tallest, as Somalis are a tall people. Customs went smoothly. Was someone here paving the way for my easy access? If so, I couldn't see them. As I was moving through customs, I was scanning the area for my possible ride into the city, but no one looked familiar, and no one came forward to claim me.

I was now outside the terminal, sitting on my equipment cases and luggage. It was about 3 p.m. I was so obviously out of place and vulnerable that I began to get nervous. There was no one and no way to call anyone to notify of my arrival. I'd left that to The Hunger Project personnel who assured me I would be taken care of; they'd never given me reason to doubt their planning. But still, I waited. Eventually a white man in an old pickup truck drove by for the second time. This time he stopped and asked me if I was with that group from The Hunger Project. "Yes," I said. "Are you here to pick me up?"

"No," he answered, "but I know where you are supposed to go, and I'll get you there." And then he added, "A little dangerous to wait here by yourself, mate." His name was Billy. He was Australian and was working for Save the Children. Billy helped get my gear in his truck, and for the first time I felt I was safely on my way. Turns out I landed a day earlier than anyone had expected, and had Billy not shown up, I would have sat there until dusk or until some Somali had taken pity on me—or maybe something worse. After all this—the flights, the waiting, and the uncertainty of finding my way to where I needed to be—I was exhausted. But my day was far from over.

Billy was full of information, and some of it disturbed me. It seemed the whole country knew of John's arrival and his itinerary. If Billy knew, then it would be easy to conclude that certain anti-American factions, of which there were many, would also know. They were the guys looking for some international headlines and, I might add, they were also the guys with the guns.

After about a ten-minute drive through the dusty roads of Mogadishu and getting to know Billy along the way, we arrived at a high-walled compound. After beeping twice, the gate opened. I was shown the apartment where our advance crew was staying and unloaded my gear inside. There was no sign of Charlie Duell, our advance man for The Hunger Project and the guy who was supposed to arrange my pickup from the airport. But what looked like his suitcase was there, so I crashed on one of the cots and waited. Billy thought they'd be along soon and told me I'd be safe here until they returned.

Sure enough, Charlie arrived within the hour and was completely dumbstruck that I was there already and about how I managed to find my way to him. I told him the story and was finally at ease about where I was. There was a big problem lurking, however, and he needed me to help him figure it out. John and the crew flying in from Burkina Faso couldn't get in until the evening, and the airport shut down at sunset. The airport had lights, but because the airspace above Mogadishu was now militarized and for recent security reasons, they would not turn them on. Planes did land there at night on occasion so we knew it was possible, but we were going to have to persuade someone to keep the lights on so our plane could land. It was already about 5 p.m., and we needed to find out who we could contact to get permission to turn the lights on.

If there's one thing I've learned traveling in developing nations, it's that a little US currency can open a lot of closed doors. I suggested driving back to the airport and persuading with gifts whomever was running the tower to turn the lights on. We purchased a carton of European cigarettes from a store and headed back to the airport. Luckily, there was just one guy in charge of the tower, and he could turn on the runway lights. The cigarettes were nice, but the $50 cinched the deal. But there was a caveat. He would only turn them on once the tower had made radio contact and he could see our plane's landing lights. This would most likely mean that they would have to make their approach, pass the runway, and then make a second approach once they had lights to guide them in.

It was now after 8 p.m. The sun had set long ago, and the moonless sky was clear but dark. I was standing on the warm asphalt tarmac staring up at the empty sky. Hours before, I was standing close to this very spot surrounded by Somalis busily making their way through customs. But now there was no one to be seen. The airport was dark and silent except for one light in the control tower and the voices of Charlie and the control tower operator. The silence and darkness, along with the warmth of the evening, made the night dreamlike. The window of the tower was open, so Charlie could hear me when I signaled to him that I saw the plane. Those wrecked planes, just a few yards away, stood like ghosts from the past, adding to the eeriness of the evening.

The plan was that Charlie would stay in the tower to hear when our pilot made radio contact. That would signal to me when I should start looking for the lights of the plane. Unlike looking in the night sky in the United States, where you can see several planes at any given moment, the sky over Somalia was completely empty of aircraft, so seeing our plane should be easy. I could hear the radio, and Charlie indicated how far out they were. Soon I saw the blinking red and green lights as the runway lights began to flicker on. Our plane flew overhead, banked a turn, and then approached.

There is no way to describe the joy I felt seeing that plane in the night sky. It was as if I had been abandoned on a desert island and for the first time saw my rescuers approaching by ship!

Wheels down and I heard a shout from Charlie, who was as excited as I was to have helped bring them in safely. Once the plane was off the runway and on the tarmac, the runway lights went immediately dark. A bus approached from the tarmac gate to take everyone to the hotel, its headlights the only light now visible. Where were these guys this afternoon when I was sitting outside looking for a ride? All of a sudden, we seemed organized and properly prepared. . . . It's a good feeling when you have the people and the proper papers all in order when traveling in a developing nation. Relying on your instincts is a little scary and often downright dangerous.

John greeted me with a big smile as he got off the plane and told me he was glad I was back, which I took to mean that he wasn't all that thrilled with taking direction from George. George greeted me with pretty much the same message. Both indicated that they did get some interesting stuff on tape, which made me feel good. Everyone looked exhausted and in need of a shower. They had flown in from tiny Burkina Faso, a landlocked country in sub-Saharan Africa, where the crew slept outside on mats and hadn't showered.

We packed ourselves and the equipment into a van and a few minutes later we were in town at our hotel. On the outside, it was an impressive structure built in 1928 in the classic Moroccan style. It sat on a little peninsula by the sea next to a castle tower that sat up against the breakwater. When we arrived at night, with the windows open and the breeze blowing, it seemed very serene. At one time, it was Somalia's only five-star hotel, but it had seen better days. Originally owned and operated by an Italian family, it had since been taken over and was now run by the government, and things were deteriorating on the inside. If you had a choice, you wouldn't stay. But we had no choice. Given the late hour, there was really no alternative, so we each found our room to get some sleep. I'd now been up for at least twenty-four hours, much of it emotionally exhausting, and I was dog-tired.

My room was on the first floor across the hall from George. We agreed to keep all the equipment in one room with George and decided to always have someone in the room with the equipment as insurance against theft. One look at my room, and I knew I would not be sleeping there. On the floor were four dead cockroaches, each the size of my open hand. The room smelled of pesticide, so I assumed the cockroaches were an ongoing issue. George's room had no cockroaches and the water worked in his bathroom. Not so in mine, so we agreed to share the room at least for the night. I took a walk out to the lobby to find Joan, John, and Charlie discussing alternative hotel arrangements. Obviously, they had seen their accommodations. I was thrilled to hear it, but it was late, and we were going to have to get through this first night at the Al-Uruba.

As I got into bed, the sheets felt damp and smelled like mildew. The sea, just a few yards out our window, kept everything damp. Although the sound of the surf was welcome, the humidity it created was not. Welcome to Somalia! George, with whom I had traveled all over the United States on various video shoots, took it all in stride, and somehow his tolerance of the situation made it palatable—a big reason why I chose him for this project. We both found the humor in the situation and found a way to finally fall asleep.

I was up at dawn. I might have slept three hours, but it was enough. I was excited to get the day going. Whatever was on the schedule today, I was sure it would be an adventure. I made my way to the hotel lobby to see if there were any options for breakfast. George agreed to stay with the equipment and then take his turn out. In the daylight, and after some sleep, the hotel looked more impressive. It was like being on set in the movie *Casablanca*.

Everywhere there were huge arched windows and doors, thick flowing Arabic draperies—but all of it aged and in poor repair. I walked toward the sound of native Somalis talking and entered the hotel cafe to find a sea of white-robed Muslim men meeting with each other, drinking tea. I was surely a standout in my jeans, Nike shoes, and red polo shirt. Feeling every eye on me, I passed through the cafe hoping to find a familiar face that might help me navigate my way to some sort of breakfast. Either none of my party were up yet or no one was interested in exploring, so I went it alone.

Outside it was already warm. The sun was bright in a cloudless sky. The grounds of the hotel were impressive. You can tell that this was once the jewel of Somalia tourism, a suitable meeting place for eastern African elite and foreign dignitaries. On this day, its shimmer had certainly faded, but then so had the rest of life in Mogadishu. There were no new structures anywhere, no signs of progress or improvement. This once proud hotel was dying a slow death, and that, I would discover, was the story of all of Somalia.

You don't take an international celebrity like John Denver to a place like Somalia without doing some serious reconnaissance. Had John not been an ambassador for UNICEF, our trip would not have taken place. This title afforded him the protection of the UN. Although a UN representative did not always travel with us, there was one in every country, each ensuring our safety as we navigated our way across the continent. That was great for John, but it did not mean the film crew, who often traveled alone without John, were assured the same safety.

The UN guys stuck with John, and as long as we were all together, we were reasonably safe. However, there were days when we were off on our own and solely at the mercy of our guides and drivers. And it was on such a day that our film crew ran into trouble.

Before all that though, my morning exploration took me around the hotel and out into the street. A block down the street from the hotel was a bank that I was told would exchange US dollars for Somalia currency. Making my way there, I encountered street vendors, tailors, and little huts that sold electronics—mostly transistor radios, watches, and jewelry.

Near the bank sat a horribly disfigured old man, begging. It reminded me of stories I had heard from other places I'd visited, that a family would purposely break or distort the legs of a child to ensure that child had some form of income in later years as a beggar. Imagine the desperation of a family who would do that to their child, in a twisted act of compassion for his or her future. Such is life in many places on our planet.

It was still early, but the bank had opened. I didn't have to exchange many of my US dollars, as it seemed Somalia currency was pretty useless. I traded what I felt I would need for the next few days and headed back to the hotel. Upon my arrival was the good news that we were moving to a different hotel, and by 10 a.m., Range Rovers were outside waiting for us.

A few minutes later, we arrived at the Caesar del Sud Hotel in downtown Mogadishu. It was simple but clean and free from cockroaches. The toilets worked, and the water stayed on all day. Perfect!

The Caesar del Sud was owned by Italians and was the hardest hotel to get into because it was small and had better security than most other hotels. It had double doors and an armed security officer. We had to double up for the two nights we would be there, so George and I, plus all the equipment, would share a room.

The Caesar also had a restaurant that was reportedly safe, but I didn't think I would be eating there. I'd packed a week's supply of nuts, trail mix, and protein bars, figuring that the food situation in Somalia would be iffy at best and so, up until this point, I had stuck with eating my own stash. Others in our group were more adventurous and, as it turned out, the food at the hotel was okay. I tried the chicken. It was a scrawny piece of meat and oddly prepared, so I just concentrated my efforts on the bread and vegetables. You can't go wrong with bread! That, as it turned out, was the only meal I felt was safe enough to eat in Somalia.

On this, the first full day here, the plan was to take my crew (without John, Joan, or The Hunger Project group) out to advance our next day's shooting and get some B-roll footage at the same time. We had two Range Rovers. The first, driven by our guide, had George, Werner, me, and all our equipment. In the second was Bilge (pronounced *Bil-geh*, a Circassian American woman who spoke the language and was versed in the local customs and culture), our grip Jim Jack, a man from the Somali National Refugee Commission, and our driver.

Because it was a long drive, we were all prepared to spend the night and wait for John and the others to arrive in the morning. This plan did not thrill me. It would leave my crew separated from the people and papers we needed in case something went wrong, an eventuality I wanted to be prepared for. But being assured that armed security would be present, I agreed to the plan. Our destination that day was the refugee camp at Qoryoley, which was about twenty minutes outside of the ancient port town of Merca. Near Merca was the Sambusa, a seaside restaurant and hotel where we would spend the night. Sounded intriguing, maybe even romantic. It was not.

A word about armed security: The quality of trusted security in many developing nations is directly related to the amount of cash said security is paid. Their devotion and attendance to your security can easily be derailed by a better offer. These are not military police bound by a greater calling or military code of conduct. They are similar to the Hells Angels, contracted by the day to protect you. This is why having people and papers is so important. Someone whom every faction recognizes as an authority (such as a UN representative with all the proper Somalia permits) would be recognized as a neutral authority to be respected. Our US passports and a good story and smile would not.

Merca was on our way to Qoryoley, so we decided to check out our accommodations for the night while the sun was still up, knowing that it would be a long day and our arrival time would be uncertain. My driver pointed to the Sambusa as we approached, and I scanned the area he was pointing at only to find a few canvas huts with thatched roofs surrounded by vacant land.

No way this looked safe to me. I told the crew, let's go and check it out before we make any plans to spend the night. There was no hotel building.

There were maybe twenty huts, and each would sleep two people. The baths were outdoors and the toilet communal, which was typical for this part of the world in those days. It was only for one night, so I put it to a vote. George was the only yes, which I knew he would be. I could live with the spartan accommodations, and I didn't relish driving back to Mogadishu by dark of night, but my gut was saying that staying would be a worse idea, given the lack of security and access to safe food and water.

I might have found this a quaint little spot interesting for an evening, but with a crew and equipment to protect and no real security possible, I decided we'd go back to Mogadishu and drive out with John and the others in the morning. I could tell my crew was relieved, and by the end of this day we would all have realized how unsafe it would have been to stay.

We were to meet the representatives from the Qoryoley refugee camp here to be escorted into the camp, but they were nowhere in sight. It was midafternoon, and we had the choice to either drive into the camp unescorted or turn back to Mogadishu to ensure our arrival before dark. Dark is not a good time to travel in Somalia with a film crew and lots of expensive equipment. Actually, daylight isn't all that safe either, but because everybody is busy going on with their business, it's easier to move around undetected. No one is out at night, but if someone is, local militia will view them as suspects to search, and that process rarely ends without delay, or worse. I decided to err on the side of safety and turn back. Where we were right then, however, was loaded with local color, and George decided he wanted to capture some of this on tape, so he was already pulling out the camera. We were situated on the coast of the Indian Ocean. If you took away the poverty all around us, the landscape was beautiful and made for some spectacular video.

We took a short walk down to the beach. It was breathtaking. Anywhere else in the world, this beach would be littered with big hotels and mobs of tourists. Here, it was pristine with no sign of commercialism, no cars, and no people except one lone local couple walking along the shoreline. They struck an impressive silhouette against the sun-soaked sky through George's video lens.

Technically, we didn't have permission to shoot anywhere outside of the refugee camps, but with our local guides acting as lookouts for any officials who might get nosey, we shot whatever and wherever we wanted without hassle. On the drive out earlier, we shot an amazing scene of a camel herd, easily two miles long, with hundreds of camels being herded by just three men on camels themselves. Every few miles, you happened upon a scene you could only imagine from something you'd seen or read in *National Geographic*. Surprises awaited around every corner. While driving to Qoryoley, we happened upon a gorgeous Somali woman walking along the road, easily six feet tall in her brightly colored wrap. She was miles from anywhere looking like she had just walked out of the pages of *Vogue* magazine.

With the shadows beginning to lengthen and facing a long drive back to Mogadishu, I instructed the crew to pack up for the drive back. George kept the camera on his lap for any opportunities we'd encounter on the way.

As our two-vehicle convoy wove its way through the narrow streets of Merca on its way out of the port town, we suddenly noticed we were being closely followed, and just as suddenly we were surrounded by a truckload of militia soldiers signaling us to pull over. The dozen soldiers sitting in the back of the truck all fanned out to create a perimeter around us, and their senior officer began to engage in a loud conversation with Bilge, our local translator. We all stayed still so as not to provoke any additional inspection. After a brief argument (which Bilge seemed to be losing), she approached our vehicle to inform us that we were being summoned to the local police compound until our permits could be properly reviewed. This was not good news. The one thing we all feared most—being detained in a Somali jail— was perhaps close to happening.

We had no choice but to follow our new militia friends to their police headquarters. As my mind raced, I clung to the one thing I thought would help—we had the right people and papers with us: Bilge and our Somali drivers. We should be able to talk our way out of whatever the issue was.

Still, we were all scared. In this adrenaline-filled moment, something told me to have George remove the videotape cassette from the camera (which had much of the day's footage on it) and hide it in one of our bags, and then replace it with a blank tape. My thinking was that if they wanted the tape for some reason, we could use it to bargain our way out of the situation. Going through the motion of removing it from the camera and handing it to them might be compelling enough to convince them that we were harmless. I had no idea why we were being investigated, but I knew we were in a Muslim country where they were sensitive about photography and thought that might be the reason. I also knew that there was no way they could view the blank tape we would give them. I was sure there wasn't a Beta SP video machine in that country on which it could be watched, except ours. I just had to keep my fingers crossed that, if it came to it, turning it over to them would be enough.

The police compound in Merca was an intimidating place. High walls, lots of barbed wire, and way too many armed soldiers in camouflage uniforms for our comfort.

We entered a small room about twenty feet square with a long table in the middle. Four senior officers sat behind in folding chairs. The desk was empty of any papers or files that you'd expect to see. There was a great deal of shouting as we were escorted into the room and instructed where to stand. George was with me on one end, holding the camera. He whispered to me on the way in asking if I wanted to record our interrogation. He knew I knew what he meant: He could turn on the tape recorder, and although we would keep the lens cap on the camera, at least we could get the audio of the meeting. I said no. It seemed that we were in enough trouble already and if they happened to see the little red LED light on the camera, we would really be in trouble. And if we ended up giving them the tape, it wouldn't do us any good anyway.

Bilge and the interrogation panel argued for twenty minutes, mostly in Somali, but the gist of the problem was exactly what I had thought: We had offended them by shooting our cameras without permission. They all spoke some English, so I chimed in at the right moment and made my offer of apology and asked if I might present them with the videotape so they would know that none of the footage would leave the country. They protested. Leaving them the tape and the camera would be acceptable, however. There was no way that was going to happen, I said to myself, but at least I now knew we could negotiate our way out of this. I explained, and Bilge interpreted. We had many more countries to visit, and we were here at great expense; losing the camera would make our trip useless. We were here under sanction from the UN, and they were involved in the production of our film (a bit of a white lie). I couldn't recall what else I said, but the UN thing, which I'm sure Bilge relayed to them as well, seemed to get some traction. And then silence. There was a little mumbling among themselves, which, by watching their stares at George and me, said we might be the focus of their irritation. They stood, nodded, and agreed to let us go. They would keep the tape and review it (I can't imagine how), and we promised to deliver them proper permits on our return trip tomorrow. We sighed in relief and made our way out of the compound.

But, not so fast. As we headed out of town, we were again followed and then ordered to turn around and return to the police compound. The same camouflaged militia led the way. Now I was scared. I had no other chips to offer in further negotiations and our being summoned back this late in the afternoon could only mean someone higher up thought we got away too easily. Again, we were led into the same room in front of the same panel of authorities. This time, however, there was an additional man, in civilian clothes, barking orders at everyone. He was the chief of police in this town. He also was the man we shot video of that afternoon who was walking with his wife along the beach.

He was angry at his men for letting us go, and he was angry at our crew for filming the private moments with his wife. I explained how we were not interested in showing him and his wife specifically, how having the sun behind him only made them silhouettes, and how they were so far away no one could possibly recognize who they were. Besides, I had given the tape to them anyway. This explanation fell on deaf ears, and I decided the best thing now would be to stay quiet and let him vent. And vent he did. When in this kind of situation, regardless of where you are, it's best to let the shouting continue if it seems contained, as vocal abuse is often a replacement for physical abuse.

An hour went by. At one point, more armed men came into the room and stood by the two doors out. This was not an encouraging sign. Bilge tried as best she could to intervene as the panel each took turns with their inquisitional accusations and harangues. But she and our guides were verbally abused as lackeys of these foreign, law-breaking, possibly spying Americans. When Bilge translated that little tidbit of information, my heart skipped a beat. I realized we were going to be there for a while.

When those on the panel each had their say, the room suddenly became quiet. The chief of police asked Bilge for the letter she carried, a work permit of sorts for the crew issued by the Somali government. The work permit should have been accompanied by the film permit, but it was not. I held my breath as first he studied it and then angrily slid it over the desk back to her and reminded her that tomorrow she would deliver the permit for his inspection. She agreed, and he silently waved us out of the room.

"We're free to go?" I asked Bilge. "I guess," she replied. We hustled out to our vehicles. People and papers saved the day. Without Bilge and the papers we did have, who knows what would have happened to us. There was a mistrust of Americans in general and the press in particular. But having our papers let this authority know that someone would be looking for us if we didn't return safely, and that was enough to save us from any further action.

It was now getting dark. The police truck with all the soldiers accompanied us out of the village so we either wouldn't get lost, or worse, make a wrong turn into more trouble.

Back in Mogadishu, everything was status quo. No one was expecting us back, so no one was worried that we were now navigating our way to the hotel in the dark, something we had explicitly been warned to avoid at all costs. There were no phones to call or even a two-way radio to signal John and the rest of our party in Mogadishu of our situation, so we just proceeded as quickly as possible, hoping to avoid some of the militia roadblocks that probably were between us and safety.

As a precaution, we hid the camera and equipment under the backpacks and blankets we'd stored in the back of our Range Rover. The Range Rover without all the equipment drove ahead of us. If we got stopped, Bilge, who was in the first vehicle, might be able to talk our way through the roadblock, and they might take a look in her vehicle, which was empty. Knowing we were together, they just might wave us through. It didn't take long to test our plan.

Out in the middle of the road, miles from any town or village, we were stopped at a roadblock. Two armed soldiers began to search both vehicles from the outside. I heard Bilge conferring with a third. He accepted her explanation and off we went to the next roadblock a few miles ahead.

Having gotten through the first roadblock was apparently good enough for the militia at the second roadblock, and they waved us through without any hassle. The temperature outside was mild, and the countryside under the light of the stars was beautiful and serene. One wonders how wonderful this place must have been before the greed and power struggles of warring tribes.

After an hour, we saw the soft lights of Mogadishu. The moonless night sky was dark. The city at night was dim. There were no neon or bright lights. The city was sprawling, but not tall. Few buildings along the skyline were more than three stories high. Although not technically under the curfew of martial law, it was understood that nothing good happens at night and the streets were empty of both people and cars. It was a relief to be this close to having the day behind us.

Without a guide, anyone would be lost in Mogadishu. Signage was virtually nonexistent. And there were no streetlights to guide the way. As we entered a town just outside of the city, we made a wrong turn directly into four armed soldiers guarding a closed gate. They immediately raised their rifles, aiming them at our heads. My window was down and the business end of a soldier's AK-47 assault rifle was six inches from my right eye. At least two of us said "Shit" at exactly the same time, as the soldiers jerked open the doors and demanded we get out of the vehicle. We were told to line up facing the closed gate with our hands behind us. We heard them talking as they rummaged through the vehicle.

Our guides, while explaining what we were doing and where we were going, were trying to derail any further harm. We were told to turn around, then signaled to return to the vehicle. We found everything intact. One soldier had my protein bar, which was in a bag of fruit and nuts, in his mouth. We said thank you and got the hell out of there. Our other vehicle, which had been behind us since our last stop, was nowhere in sight. Presumably, they had seen our wrong turn and decided not to make the same mistake.

Shaken and dead tired from the exhausting emotional stress of the day, we grabbed our gear and said goodbye to our guides for the night knowing the next day we'd have to repeat the route, this time with John along. We arrived at our hotel just minutes later than the other vehicle, but the news of our ordeal had already found John, Joan, and the others, who were waiting for us in the lobby. They called a meeting of all the crew to get the story and to try to plan for either an early departure from Somalia or to figure out a safer plan for getting the footage we needed. I argued for staying, reasoning that what had happened to us most likely would clear the way for us tomorrow, as long as we made good on our promise to return with proper permits.

The next day John would be with us, so there would be at least four vehicles and one UN representative, which would lessen the likelihood of having the same unfortunate events happen again. Mogadishu had an ample supply of nongovernmental organizations (NGO), and The Hunger Project knew them all, so some of those staff members were called to join our meeting. They were amused by our story as if to say, *Did you think you were traveling to Palm Springs?* "This is Somalia, man," somebody said. "Battlefield Somalia." Bilge and one of the NGO guys suggested driving out early the next morning to visit with the regional governor to smooth the way for our next day's trip, and then proceed to Merca to present the permits. The rest of us—John, Joan, and the crew—would drive out a couple hours later. We all agreed and headed back to our rooms.

George, who has got to be the easiest traveling companion of all time, seemed completely unaffected by the day's events and quickly fell asleep. I would have liked to talk about it awhile, just to make sure we witnessed the same thing, but instead, I made some notes so I could one day tell it as accurately as it happened.

But there was to be one more unplanned adventure for me. Between our meeting the night before and the new sunrise, some unexplained event happened. I heard about it at 7 a.m. when I got a knock on my door. Jon Duell, one of The Hunger Project staff members, told me that I was to go with him to see the regional governor as quickly as I could get dressed. The governor wanted to talk with whoever was the person in charge of the filming. "Just the two of us?" I asked. "No, just you. But I'm going with you."

By this time, I couldn't wait to get out of this country.

Within the hour, I was in a car heading to a house that was perched on top of a little hill and surrounded by a high wall. As we drove up, a gate opened to let us in. There was, of course, security everywhere. I had by this time given myself over to the fact that whatever we did or wherever we went in this country, we would be encountering some armed resistance. I didn't even worry on my drive about what might happen to me, because there was nothing I could do about it. We were welcomed into what we learned was the regional governor's residence. The governor was getting ready to see us and would be out in a moment. Would we like some tea? Sure. So, Jon Duell and I were in Somalia in what must be the governor's living room sipping tea. It was by far the nicest room I'd been in since entering Somalia. What might pass for a modest middle-income home in the States was a mansion here.

When the governor made his way into the room, we both stood up. It took all my strength of character not to laugh, though, as the governor was in his full military outfit, with all the ribbons and badges adorning his chest. He looked like photos I'd seen of Idi Amin. As it turned out, he was a most gracious host. He had asked us to his home in hopes of explaining the problems facing his country these days. He spoke in heavily accented English, but we understood every word. It wasn't long before I realized this meeting was to accept his apology for the way we were treated the day before. I was humbled by his demeanor and sincerity. Our meeting lasted about a half hour, and, as he requested, I gave him a rundown of the day's schedule. He wanted to meet me, I'm sure, because he felt I was the storyteller in the group, and he wanted to make sure we understood that

Somalia was a great country, rich with heritage and would be great again, in spite of its current political problems.

He shook our hands as if to say no hard feelings, and suggested that today might go more smoothly for us. It certainly did.

I don't know what transpired overnight that led to this shift in accommodation with the local authorities, but whatever it was, it worked wonders for us with regard to access. We now roamed quite freely through the territory we had covered the day before, this time without incident. By late morning we were at the Qoryoley refugee camp a short distance inland from Merca. Someone must have either tipped off the local police officials that we were free to gather the footage we needed, or someone delivered the permits as we had promised. Either way, everyone seemed to be on the same page now, and although we frequently encountered the police or militia, they left us to our business.

Upon arriving at the refugee camp, we were assigned a guide: an Ethiopian man of nineteen who was close to seven feet tall. He had walked from Ethiopia into Somalia with his family to escape the civil war and starvation, a distance of over two hundred miles. Every one of his family members, save for him, had been lost to starvation and disease along the way.

Everywhere you looked and every face you saw bore the scars of hunger and suffering. It's no wonder our cameras were not welcomed by the established authorities. They knew it was virtually impossible to portray this country in a positive light. And when looking at the country from a wide angle, they were right. John was visibly shaken by the enormity of the suffering we saw. But as he would remind us, the purpose of our trip to Africa was to find and document what was working in the fight against the persistence of hunger. Clearly, if we found something working in Somalia, it was going to be on the micro level, with individual successes.

For the first time, the crew and John were together and at a location where we could get some useful footage. I had to structure our shooting around each location in real time, as we really had no one qualified to advance locations, and even if we had, the dynamics of each location changed dramatically from day to day, hour to hour. I tried to arrange each day with several setups featuring John, speaking to the camera in somewhat generic terms, and then relied on all the extensive B-roll footage we shot to tell the story. We tried to include John in the B-roll footage as much as possible to place him in the proper context with his on-camera narrative. We found, however, that it was much easier to work apart from him, as all the activity surrounding his movement through a location was distracting.

Few of the Somalis, if any, really knew who John Denver was, but because of security and the attention he received by the non-Somalis with him, it was easy to conclude this visitor was a celebrity of some sort.

Being in the refugee camp was the one thing I most dreaded when we were planning our trip. As I had mentioned earlier, I knew the idea of seeing children starving would really affect me emotionally, and I thought I might have difficulty concentrating on what I needed to accomplish as I shot the film. As it turned out, those fears were unfounded.

If you had looked at the camp from the air, it would have been a sea of tents. There were hundreds of tents along row after row of access roads—makeshift boulevards of sorts. There were vendors and markets and schools. There were dining locations, freshwater reservoirs, and sanitation areas. There were hospital tents for the sick and most severely malnourished, trade schools for both men and women, and relocation services. Most of the population here was from Ethiopia, innocent victims of their country's civil war. Most were happy to be in the camp, living in relative safety until they could relocate back to their homes. Many would stay on in Somalia or move farther south to neighboring Kenya. Because the mass migration out of Ethiopia had slowed, the camp had more of a lived-in feel. Most had been here awhile, regained their health, and (thanks to the massive efforts of food aid organizations like CARE, Catholic Relief Services, World Vision, and other nonprofit organizations) were now receiving daily meals or dietary supplies to make meals for their families.

Everywhere you went in the camp, a cadre of children followed you. They didn't beg or ask for anything. They were just curious about us and what we were doing in their camp. For a child who had been asked to travel hundreds of miles from his or her home by foot to a strange land, witnessing untold hardships, if not atrocities, along the way, I supposed the relative stability of camp life was a welcome change. They certainly did not lack for friends as there were many more children than adults. Children were the most populous group in the camp, followed by adult women, and lagging far behind, adult men. Most of the men had either died on the trip to the camp or were casualties of war in Ethiopia.

We were in Africa to document what was working in the fight to eliminate the persistence of hunger. The camp obviously was not a long-term solution, but it was a way station of sorts between starvation and the possibilities of a new start and self-sustainment. If the camp provided the knowledge and tools necessary to facilitate a family's fresh start when it was time to relocate, then the process would be a success. This camp seemed to be a good model to meet that end.

John was deeply moved by what he witnessed there. Although we were all prepared for the visuals, our eyes only saw part of the story. The sounds, the smells, the temperature, the dust, the burning sun, and the warm wind completed it. None of us were prepared for the enormity of the camp or the immense infrastructure required to keep it working. It seemed to go on for miles, and every family tent we passed on our way across the camp housed a gripping story of survival, and multiplied by thousands, it seemed unimaginable even though it was right in front of our eyes. For John it was personal. Several times, as we were scouting the next setup, he would wander off into the dust to greet the people there, mostly children. I think it really struck him, as it did all of us—the vastness of the problem and the effort it would take to solve it. It wasn't academic any longer; it was personal, and it was painful.

We only had a few short hours to film. Joan and The Hunger Project folks really did not want us to concentrate too much time on the camp for the reasons I mentioned earlier. It was not so much a solution as a much-needed Band-Aid. It wasn't really the focus of our purpose, but it was necessary to witness it as one of the responses to mass hunger and starvation. We shot a great deal of footage anyway, and then we made a mad dash back to Mogadishu to board our plane to Zimbabwe before darkness fell. This time we had a police escort to smooth the way. We were told our hotel in Harare, Zimbabwe, our next destination, was modern.

They would have phone service there. I was anxious to call home and tell my story, but when I finally did call Deb, I left out the guns and jailhouse part so she wouldn't worry. And I would still have two more weeks to add to it anyway. I could hear Tyler in the background giggling.

A quote from the travel advisory I read sometime later warned: "Do not travel to any part of Somalia because there is armed conflict, the ongoing very high threat of terrorist attack or kidnapping, and dangerous levels of violent crime. If you are in Somalia, leave if it is safe to do so." No kidding!

There were many other memorable moments from this trip to Africa apart from the dramatic days in Somalia, some of which were pure fun. Martin Luther King III was on our trip because his mother was a consultant for The Hunger Project and wanted her son to see the realities of the problem. Martin was a polite young man who loved basketball. We connected on this subject, as I had played basketball since my teens. When we were in Zimbabwe during this trip, Martin and I somehow found ourselves working out with the Zimbabwe Olympic basketball team! Not sure who set it up or how we managed it, but we actually scrimmaged with African players late one evening.

Our days in Zimbabwe were the most fun, the wind down of our arduous three-week tour. On one of our last nights in Zimbabwe, we were staying at the historic Victoria Falls Hotel. We ate dinner together at one long table while a band played reggae music. John, who had several glasses of wine, was invited to join the band—which he did—and sang a couple of reggae tunes much to our amusement. After dessert, he asked George and me if we would accompany him on a walk to Victoria Falls. The night was warm, and the moon was full. Unlike the Grand Canyon, there are no man-made rails or fences of any sort on the high cliffs surrounding the falls. John sat on a rocky ledge, obviously drunk and unstable, soaking in the beauty of our surroundings. I quietly told George to hook a finger in John's belt loop, as I was doing on the other side. John only realized this when he got up. But we were afraid that he might plummet to his death. He was always fearless, but that night he seemed a bit jumpy too, leaping from slippery rock to rock, declaring what a billy goat he was. With that, it became clear he had consumed more than just wine at dinner. The walk back to the hotel was just as telling: a sloppy, slurred collection of remorse and loss he felt about his separation from Annie and the kids. If ever you are going to feel homesick, Africa is the place.

But those last days in Africa also revealed John's amazing ability to reach out and communicate across ethnic boundaries and language barriers. One morning, we boarded a couple of small planes and flew into a barren part of central Zimbabwe to document a farm project. It was a very remote and underdeveloped part of the country, but this little village had managed to create a successful community farm. We landed hard on a short dirt airstrip. It was pretty typical weather in central Africa, warm and clear, and, as always, we didn't know what the day might bring.

The local community leaders and village elders welcomed us. We always drew a crowd, being a bunch of Americans with cameras. We were then escorted to the village, where about a hundred villagers greeted us, mostly women and children, and sang and danced to their native songs. It was a beautiful sight rarely seen by tourists. They encircled us and sang as they bounced up and down in their long, brightly colored clothing. It was a song of welcome, and, although we couldn't understand the lyrics, the communication was clear. We were given a tour of the community farm, where we shot a lot of film. We were about to leave when John got word that a group of children wanted us to see their school. They were very proud of their little schoolhouse, which they had rebuilt after the war for independence a few years earlier. It was late, and we were urged to get back to the airstrip, but John couldn't turn them down, so we stopped by the school. It was a modest little two-room schoolhouse by our standards, but it was the pride of their community.

The children had no idea who John Denver was. They lived in an isolated, remote part of the world with no electricity or modern conveniences, and they spoke only their own language. Most hadn't ever been more than a few miles from their home village, and there was no city of any size for a hundred miles. They congregated around us all not knowing who the focus of attention should be. Then John leaned into the Range Rover we'd arrived in and grabbed his guitar. He stood in the middle of all the kids, ranging in age from about six to sixteen, and pulled his guitar strap over his shoulder. The kids went silent. John began to sing "Sunshine on My Shoulders." The children had no idea what the lyrics were, but they were completely taken with the music. It was pure communication from one heart to another, and these children, unspoiled by material possessions or the politics of the planet, fully received it. You could see it in their eyes, and you could feel it in the air.

This was the very essence of what John and his music were about. At the end of the song, they didn't know to clap. They just stared, as if to say, "Don't stop." So John sang "Annie's Song." The kids didn't move a muscle. And then we had to leave. As John made his way back to our vehicle, the children got closer, touching John and his guitar as if in a big group hug, wanting to hear more. But we were losing light and the planes would wait no longer, so the moment ended. And we all got a glimpse of what John always preached—that music transcends politics, culture, even language, and touches, heart to heart. This would be our final day with the people of Africa.

Flying back to Paris in our private jet, the mood was pensive. The comfort and luxury of that jet was now something to both appreciate and ponder. We, as a nation, regardless of our personal financial status, are so incredibly blessed. It takes a trip like we just endured to fully appreciate the scope of that blessing—and the responsibility to serve that comes with it. None of this was lost on our crew, particularly John, and I think how each of us was now dealing with this new reality was the reason that little plane cabin was so quiet.

Somewhere along our route home, Jon Duell asked me for my suit size. A request of the privileged coming from where we were. As it turned out, he needed to rent me a tux for a banquet they wanted me to attend at the Waldorf Astoria on the night of our return to New York. That event was a true culture shock. Still getting the dust out of my eyes from weeks in sub-Saharan Africa, I found myself at a lavish banquet table, sipping a full-bodied cabernet in a room packed with tuxedo- and gown-clad celebrities and dignitaries. Sitting directly across from me at my table was artist Andy Warhol. His stare reminded me that I was truly out of my element.

A day ago, I had been in a world where hunger and starvation were life's reality. Now I was dining with kings. It was hard to sit at that meal and not at least tear up from the mixed emotions that juxtaposition presented. John realized it, too. He walked over to our table and greeted the guests, leaned into me at my seat, and whispered, "How weird does this feel?"

In the end, our trip didn't produce the documentary I was hoping for. It served The Hunger Project with what they wanted, using segments for recruitment and fundraising purposes, but I thought we had missed a real opportunity to show the world what was working in the fight to end hunger. But what a life adventure it turned out to be.

When it was all over, I reflected on my extraordinary experiences in Africa. I was not a US service member. I was not a member of the Peace Corps. I was not a volunteer or employee of a humanitarian rescue organization. I was an employee of a major American celebrity—one with a conscience, a soul, and a determination to have a hand in addressing hunger on our planet. John's fame had created access for us. It gave us the keys to the world and an opportunity to serve.

Welcome to Windstar, Snowmass, Colorado. Photo courtesy John Denver photo archive.

Chapter 7

DENVER ENTERPRISES

If someone engages me in a conversation about my experiences with John and touring, the conversation will almost always find its way to matters of money. And, I have to admit, it is one of the more intriguing subjects. How it gets made, how it's divided up, how much trickles down to the band and crew, and what it costs to keep a tour on the road. These are all unknown to most people. Plus, it's in the back of everyone's mind who encounters a famous celebrity: I wonder what he's worth?

My answer was always "Plenty," partly because I didn't really know. Except for Hal Thau, his longtime business manager, I don't think anyone really knew John's true financial worth. I don't think John knew. And I don't think he cared that much.

When I was working full-time with John, I was paid through John Denver Concerts, Inc. I had a pension plan for all those years through both Concerts Inc. and through John Denver Enterprises. When I went off salary and on a monthly retainer, the pension plan share they paid ceased, although I was kept on the company's healthcare plan as part of my retainer.

I opted to take my pension money out of the company's program. This gave me the capital I needed to launch my new design business. What some say was a stupid move because that money could have grown substantially had I held onto it turned into a smart one: That pension fund was later transferred into the hands of a guy by the name of Bernie Madoff.

When I got news of this, it surprised me. I never saw John's fiscal manager, Hal Thau, as anything but a careful and conservative guy, and I know he truly always had John's interests at heart. It seemed out of character, which I believe speaks more to the persuasive qualities of Madoff than to the greed of Thau. But I was not there, nor was I privy to any of this as it went down. No one was. Money, the amount, where it was, and how it was invested were things nobody discussed.

John never acted like the multimillionaire he was. He was unimpressed by money but fascinated by what one could accomplish with wealth, as evidenced by the vast financial resources that went into his Windstar Foundation. He gave generously to many other charitable nonprofits, and I know he personally helped many individuals through tough times. It was usually anonymous and always without fanfare or public recognition.

I think the example that best defines John's integrity about money happened before I knew him. The Mitchell Trio had been touring for years and had been losing money for about as long. Hal Thau met John, who was a member of the group and became the group's business manager. With interest in folk trios declining quickly, Hal had to break the news that it no longer made sense for them to tour. The debt they had accumulated was into six figures and there was no way out except declaring bankruptcy and calling it a day with the trio. John refused to file the bankruptcy, instead using earnings from his meager but blossoming solo career to slowly pay off the creditors, which he finally did by the time his first hit "Leaving on a Jet Plane" had become a number one hit for Peter, Paul and Mary.

One time I was in the RCA recording studio in LA with John when he told me that he had found the Porsche he had been looking for. It was an early '60s lemon-yellow 356 Cabriolet. It was identical to the Porsche Steve McQueen's girlfriend drove in the movie *Bullitt*. Since it was in perfect condition, the asking price of $11,000 was a fair deal, if not a bargain. It was the perfect car he had been looking for. But John told me if the guy will meet him at $10,000, he was going to buy it, which cracked me up. Here was John Denver, by then a famous multimillionaire recording artist, having found the exact vintage Porsche he had been searching for, and he was quibbling with himself about spending an extra $1,000 to get it. That was vintage JD thinking.

Not that John was cheap or stingy. He was just careful in the way he would spend money on certain things. We had dinners when he spent much more than a thousand bucks on the bar tab. Sometimes logic just doesn't apply when it comes to money. He also never seemed to have cash on him. I can't tell you how many times we were together, and he'd ask if I had a twenty on me. I'm not sure if he didn't want to carry cash, or if he just forgot to get it. I never got it back from him, by the way. You would just go to Kris O'Connor and tell him, "John owes me fifty bucks." Kris would give you the cash, no questions asked. Kris was sort of like the bank on tours. When you met up with him in, say, Melbourne, he'd ask you if you needed some local money and hand you a couple hundred Australian.

The way money was handled on tour made working for the Denver organization seamlessly enjoyable. While on tour, each of us would have already received a per diem check for all our incidentals. This was to cover tips and occasional meals away from the hotel, cab rides, etc. You could bank most of it because at no time did you ever need a penny of it, except for things like tips. Flights, hotels, meals, room service, laundry service, transportation, phone calls, and so much more were included for members of John's touring company. Everything in your life on the road was taken care of. Yes, you could say we were spoiled, but we did appreciate it.

With John, I never had what anyone would consider a high-paying job. I did okay, but it was never going to be a gig I got rich from. The benefits, however, were rich indeed. First of all, I got a weekly salary. A check every week would always arrive by Wednesday. I often had months at a time when I really didn't do much of anything and still got paid. We did tour a lot in the first few years, but we never did more than 150 shows per year, which left me about half the year without an assignment.

So, I began to do projects for other acts. Everyone was beginning to want visual media for their shows. That's the thing about showbiz: Every act wants what they saw another act do, but they want to do it bigger and better. I did some music videos for Captain & Tennille, one of which had me letting ten thousand ladybugs loose in a field to film them while they did their thing. I came close to overseeing the first use of 3D visuals on a rock tour. Three Dog Night was the client. I say "close" because my proposal came at a time when the band was struggling to stay sober enough to pay the basic bills. Even though they needed a new gimmick and wanted top-level visuals, they couldn't afford the cost.

Since I was being subsidized during these off months by John, I would share the proceeds from these projects with his business. Hal once commented that for a six-month period, I was the only guy in the organization who actually generated money for them!

When I first started working with John in 1973, his fee for bringing his show to a venue in the United States was in the $15,000 to $20,000 range. And he was drawing a salary from Concerts Inc. like the rest of us. Well, not quite like the rest of us, as he was living on $10,000 a month, but, even in 1973, that was not a lot of money for an artist of his caliber. It soon changed, and by the big tour in 1975, he was making more like $35,000 to $45,000 per show, guaranteed. But because he was selling out everywhere, he usually received a percentage of the total receipts, often adding on another $15,000 to $30,000. Keep in mind that a good seat at one of those concerts was about $20. John sold a lot of concert tickets.

These numbers were not broadcast to the band and crew. I just happened to be around the promoters and was both curious and bold enough to ask the question. They usually did a quick look around to see if anyone was listening, and then whispered a number to me.

By the mid-'70s, the money was rolling in. Jerry Weintraub, John's personal manager, was booking not only John's concert tours, but also his TV and movie gigs. Jerry owned Concerts West, arguably the leading tour promotion business in the country. He also acted as producer on all of John's television specials and as executive producer of his film *Oh, God!* In his book *When I Stop Talking, You'll Know I'm Dead*, Jerry claimed there were years that he personally netted over $10 million from managing John. If true, that would mean John netted $50 million in those same years.

Jerry Weintraub was perhaps the most intriguing guy I encountered on my journey with John. He had an unwavering focus on making money, which is what made him so effective as a talent manager. When it came to bringing in the bucks, you didn't want anyone else on your side. In fact, I believe John Denver's huge national and international success is largely a credit to Jerry's savvy business management. You'll read stories in this book that showcase Jerry's unique personality, which many times seemed brazen, self-serving, and, occasionally, insulting. But he loved John and saw his unique appeal, and he was determined the entire world would see it, too.

Tall and brash, Jerry came off like a New York wiseguy. The first few times I met him, he shrugged me off like I was some crew member who would be gone tomorrow. When he began to realize that I was a fixture in the organization, he got more curious. I remember standing next to him backstage before a show he happened to attend, which was rare, and he turned and looked at me sort of from the floor up to my face and said, "Who the hell are you, anyway?" I pointed at the three screens on the stage and said, "I make that happen. My name is Lowell Norman." I put my hand out to shake hands with him. He just sort of stared for a second, sizing me up, then he took the cigar he had in his right hand and put it in his mouth, shook my hand, and mumbled, "Jerry Weintraub." This was before I had a full knowledge of who the man was and how much of John's career he orchestrated. He seemed like one of those old-time showbiz guys. You really didn't need to know anything about him to recognize he was *somebody*, as he had learned how to emit that aura of power and wealth. In so many ways he was the exact opposite of John.

I remember once while they were in casual conversation, Jerry was comparing the beauty of New York City to a redwood forest. He'd take New York every time. That was his Aspen. That was his world.

All his personality quirks aside, Jerry knew how to make money and, more importantly, he knew how to make John money. "Work it while you can" was his mantra, and keeping John working kept all of us working. John was the "engine," as he put it, but Jerry was in every way the guy behind the wheel. And with John, he had a willing and obedient partner. Kris O'Connor explained it to me this way: "You work for John. John works for Jerry."

He was trained by one of the best. Jerry Weintraub had been the protégé of Colonel Tom Parker, Elvis's manager. Jerry was able to convince Colonel Parker that he was a great promoter, so the Colonel told him that for a million dollars delivered by a certain date, he could handle Elvis's late-'60s tour, the one designed to get him back out on the road and back in the limelight. Jerry told me the story himself, and he loved doing so, as I heard him tell it a half dozen times since, and he later wrote about it in his book. Jerry and Colonel Parker never signed a contract; it was all on a handshake. Jerry took over booking, merchandising, and management of that tour. At the end of it, in San Diego, Parker took Jerry into a backstage room and had him pile the money from two large suitcases onto the table. The cash totaled in excess of $1 million. Jerry had already gotten his initial million-dollar investment back and then some, so he wasn't sure what all the cash was for. "That's all the money from the merchandising," said Colonel Parker. "Half of that is yours." He then took his cane and began to chop the pile in half. Didn't count it, just started hacking the pile into equal halves. The profits from that Elvis tour are what launched Weintraub into the concert business. He first was a manager of small nightclub acts, then a promoter, then he became a megamanager and promoter. He started Concerts West with Seattle partner Tom Hulett and never looked back.

There is something organic about talent and timing and originality; those are the fundamental makings of iconic artists who integrate into our culture by touching people with music that matters to them. Elvis Presley and John Denver are perfect examples of this, but in both cases, it also takes intelligent, thoughtful, and charismatic management to take the music and the artist to that next level of household-name status.

Jerry's significance in John's career can't be overstated, perhaps even eclipsing the influence of the Colonel's control over Elvis. John and Jerry worked well together, and they were in every sense of the word partners for a long time, all through the '70s and into the '80s.

Jerry was married to Jane Morgan, a famous singer from the late '50s and early '60s. She was a sweetheart—a real delight to know. She was Jerry's first name star he managed, and through his association with her, he began to make a name for himself in the music business. She hadn't sung for years by the time I had occasion to be around her. She had turned her focus to their growing family while Jerry became a powerful force in the music business. I liked her a lot.

I liked Jerry, too. I don't know if the word *nice* really applies when talking about him. I remember telling John once when we were driving out to Red Rocks together that I didn't know how to handle Jerry, as he was a pretty gruff guy. John assured me, "His bark is worse than his bite. You don't need to worry about him." But I did need to worry about him—he was far more professionally connected than John; I was easy to replace if I screwed up, so keeping out of his sight lines became a priority.

Eventually I developed my own relationship with Jerry, and I wound up getting along great with him. He was a larger-than-life character who was always entertaining.

Once we were in Australia at a party put on by local promoters at a ranch of some sort. There was a band playing in a barn with a huge dance floor. Touring with us was a new, young, up-and-coming singer named Debby Boone. She was in Australia as a guest on the John Denver television special we were shooting during the tour. She was a little shy, and I had worked on a couple of video shoots with her famous dad, Pat Boone. We started talking and soon discovered we had several mutual acquaintances, so we sat down at dinner together. I thought I had made a new friend. Jerry came by and said out loud, "Hey, Lowell, your wife called and wants you to call her back ASAP." Everyone sort of snickered at the obvious rudeness, but I got the message: Hands off the young lady. Jerry knew, of course, that I was not married.

Debby Boone aside, Jerry didn't like John doing things with other artists much, unless they were well-established cultural icons like Frank Sinatra. He wanted John to always be the headliner and to be his own man, another thing he learned from Colonel Parker. And the image that John Denver put out, the guy who smiled and laughed a lot and said, "Far out," was partly a creation of Jerry Weintraub. Not that there was anything fake about John Denver; far from it. But Jerry knew how to take John's own lifestyle and characteristics and showcase them as a brand that the world would love. In other words, Jerry Weintraub knew exactly who his client was: a gifted and charismatic performer with the whole entertainment package.

John was very aware of public perception of him, and if there was ever a moment of forgetfulness, Jerry Weintraub was there to remind him. He could never get too far off course with Weintraub around. John got tired of his image from time to time, wanting to change it up, maybe lose the granny glasses. Jerry would talk him out of it. You just didn't mess with the brand that was working.

Jerry wanted John's image to remain as pure as possible. John was, after all, a real live human being with that aw-shucks personality and those homespun ideals and work ethic. Jerry knew it was his job to ensure that those qualities be preserved in John Denver, the "product." I don't say that with cynicism. Jerry loved John, and he knew all those things about John to be true. But he had a job to do, and keeping the essence of John intact in his public persona was crucial to that job. Looking back, you can see his influence in the packaging of John Denver.

Other singer-songwriters of his era were packaged as more gritty, less approachable. John's album covers during the Weintraub years were more clean-cut, appealing to what Jerry referred to as a broader audience. These graphic representations of John, I believe, helped secure his image as saccharine and unsophisticated.

Having said that, one of John's most interesting albums is representative of the marketing genius of Jerry Weintraub. You would think that an album called *John Denver's Greatest Hits* would be an inevitable development, something that's thrown together after a string of radio hits. But here's the thing: John only had two hits at that time. "Rocky Mountain High" and "Take Me Home, Country Roads" were big hits for sure, but it was just those two. Jerry recognized that John was poised for a package that could expose his growing fan base to earlier songs that had been on albums that were already in the bargain bins. Also, the audacious title alone, *John Denver's Greatest Hits*, gave Jerry's client a stature that he deserved, even if the charts had only celebrated two of its eleven songs. It was like putting *best seller* on the front of a just-released book. The quality is implied right away. Jerry's philosophy was simple: If you put it out there that you have a lot of hits, then it becomes the self-fulfilling prophecy of a lot of hits.

Jerry's philosophy only works, of course, if you have the goods to back it up. He knew that John did, and the irony is that all these years later, that album really is a collection of greatest hits.

Smoke and mirrors, that's what Jerry did. The greatest hits album was a stroke of genius on his part and an artistic statement of its own from its artist. Six new versions of older songs mixed sweetly with the most recent hits. The eleven tracks flowed perfectly. This is an example of the synergy between the two friends: a businessman with an eye on navigating the commerce of music and an uncompromising artist with an eye on creative integrity. It worked. Somehow, it worked.

Once at the Forum in Los Angeles, I was sitting in the front row of the arena in front of the stage waiting for the sound check when Jerry walked over and sat one chair away smoking one of his ubiquitous cigars, with two more hanging out of his shirt pocket. I asked him what brand he was smoking. "Oh, these are Cubans. I have the Moodys or Zeppelin sneak them in when they come over to tour." Cuban cigars were of course illegal in America, but with the Moody Blues and Led Zeppelin also in his stable of artists, he could get them to score cigars when traveling abroad and smuggle them back for him in all the touring gear.

"Jeez, how much would one cost if you could buy them over here?" I asked. "Six or eight bucks," he said. This was in 1975, when six bucks could buy you a good meal. I figured he had to smoke at least a half dozen a day, more than could be stowed in some guitar cases. Doing the math in my head, I said, "Wow, are you crazy?"

"No," he said. "I'm a fucking millionaire." That story tells you about all you need to know about Jerry!

One thing I learned more about later, but only occasionally saw in action, was the infighting between Hal Thau, Milt Okun (who owned John's publishing company, Cherry Lane Music), and Jerry Weintraub. Because Jerry controlled so many aspects of John's career, Jerry demanded and received huge percentage deals on everything John did. He got half of the profits of the film *Oh, God!* and 20 to 40 percent of most everything else. Usually, a manager as creative and capable as Jerry would receive 20 to 25 percent across the board on everything. Jerry's deals were always custom, which is a nice way of saying his percentages were always higher than what other managers would receive.

In many ways he earned his keep, however outrageous it was. When John got his second deal with RCA, he was getting $7,000 advances on each album. But in the next contract after Weintraub's negotiations, he received a cool $1 million advance per album.

In those days, it was all about making and selling records. Even tours, which often just broke even, were designed to get you seen by as many record buyers as possible. A good ticket for a John Denver show then might cost $10 or $20. Today, the business model is the exact opposite of what it once was. A good seat these days, as anyone who goes to concert events will testify, can set you back $200 or more. But no one is buying albums anymore. They are buying single tracks online from iTunes for a dollar, or streaming them for free. The artists' royalties, once the backbone of a singer's financial structure, have all but crumbled.

Speaking of royalties, it's important to emphasize how publishing contributed to John's income. Milt Okun, the founder and owner of Cherry Lane Music, was an aggressive music publisher—and his most famous client, John Denver, was a prolific songwriter. Few musicians exercised all the publishing opportunities that John did. Sheet music was available for every John Denver song, and it's fair to say at least two generations of guitar players learned their instrument by strumming the chords found on John's sheet music or in one of his many music books. When you write melodic, universally loved songs based around the acoustic guitar, song publishing is an important revenue stream.

Another money stream, although not nearly as profitable, was merchandise. Merch, as we call it, was nonexistent in the early years with John. It was not until the big 1975 tour that we had anything to sell. Weintraub had some hastily designed program books that we sold on the tour for five bucks a pop. Sometime in the '80s, my design partner, Paul Hanson, and I designed a tour book that I felt better showcased the performer I knew. This set me up as the official tour program designer from then on. I made a total of seven tour books over the next twelve years. I got paid a generous flat fee on most of them for the design and printing but never margins from units sold.

Our merch guy (the guy who ran the crews that sold all our stuff at concerts) was a bit of a showbiz legend by the name of Dave Furano. Dave came to us from Weintraub's management company, Management 3. He was engaging and energetic, a wild stallion of a guy who was always thinking of ways to promote products for John, with John always pulling back on the reins. Eventually, I ended up working with Dave for Windstar Licensing, a company we formed with John and Hal. We produced environmental T-shirts, animal T-shirts, plush toys, and even a John Denver action figure. John wanted to produce products for charitable purposes too using the Newman's Own business model of Paul Newman. Our first product was a barbecue sauce of John's creation, which, by the way, was tasty on chicken. None of it went on sale because the demand wasn't there. People wanted T-shirts, hats, and program books. So, after a run of about a year with Dave, we parted company.

Profits in the merch business are an elusive thing. First of all, you need to be selling something that you cannot buy anywhere else, which is why you can charge $20 for a $3 T-shirt with John's face on it or $20 for a program book that costs $1.50 to produce. The venue, that is the stadium or theater you are occupying for the concert, gets to keep 40 to 50 percent of your net sales. So already your $20 T-shirt is really only $10 to the merchandiser. Then you have percentage royalties to give the artist for the use of his name and face on all the products. Then you have to pay your crew, and if you can't load the merch on a sound or lighting truck that's going to the next gig, you have transportation costs. It's a volume business. You have to sell a lot of merch at prices that people will pay, and the venue will accept. By the way, there is not much chance of cheating the venue on their percentage, as they count each piece before each concert and re-count each piece after. Somehow, the volume of sales usually makes it all worthwhile, but at tremendous effort.

One big seller at the merch table that John had was his *Earth Songs* CD. Produced by John for his own Windstar label, the album featured his most popular environmental songs about nature and the earth rerecorded with lush new orchestral arrangements by composer Lee Holdridge. Because you could only buy it at a concert, it was a big seller and pure profit for John because he didn't have to share any with a record company.

Another clever sales gimmick that Dave and I developed was the tree-planting project. Actually, to call it a gimmick isn't fair, because it was really an ingenious way to get concertgoers to become a part of John's vision of planting a million trees by the year 2000. We named it Plant-It 2000. For every product sold, we planted an indigenous tree in various cities where local volunteers would work with us, and with each product sold, we gave away a tree seedling in a little box. A prisoner work program in San Quentin assembled the seeds and the just-add-water mulch pellets into individual little boxes for us. We gave away thousands of them, and at one time, my garage was half full of them. My son Tyler, then six years old and daughter Lane, who was three, had quite a few giant redwood seedlings growing in our kitchen window.

Hal Thau's son Michael eventually ran Plant-It 2000, more than fulfilling John's vision of planting one million trees by the year 2000. The foundation's name was updated to Plant-It 2020 and the work continues, with millions of trees planted around the world.

John's biggest single expense, other than the land purchase and operation costs of keeping the Windstar Foundation alive, was his business jet, the Learjet 35. With a running cost of nearly $1,200 an hour, a year's worth of jet-setting meant he needed to make at least $2 million per year just to fund his preferred mode of transportation. Even though they formed a leasing company, Windstar Aviation, around the Learjet, the plane never came close to paying for itself, even when it was leased to corporate clients. After John's death, the estate had no real use for the Learjet anymore, which was brightly painted with a corporate logo and Indian motif, so they sold it. It was later sold several more times and then crashed in 2012, having slid off the runway on takeoff in Pueblo, Colorado. No one was injured.

By the end of the Weintraub-Denver relationship in the '80s, Jerry was working with Neil Diamond and Frank Sinatra, among others. He had less and less time for John, whose career was in a wholly new stage by then anyway. It couldn't have been as interesting or even as fun a relationship for either of them as it had been on the way up. Their relationship ended.

John was clearly devastated when he parted company with Jerry. I thought John would divorce his wife before even thinking of leaving Jerry, and then, surprisingly, both things happened pretty close to the same time. But John put on a brave face, always looked to the future, and always ensured those of us in his organization felt supported. In that respect, nothing changed.

Jerry was all about entertainment, and John wanted to go beyond that. He had gotten heavily involved in politics and causes by that time, an interest that Jerry didn't really share with him. Jerry had no problem with John's interest in hunger and saving the natural world, but for him, it seemed to be more about letting his star have the interests that placated him. I screened *I Want to Live*, our hunger documentary, for Jerry one evening at his Beverly Hills home. He was complimentary to me, saying this was possibly the best vehicle for John. His thinking had nothing to do with the film or the statement it made. It was purely the image of his client he was concerned about. In other words, it was all about seeing yet a different way of marketing the brand that was John Denver.

Also, by the time John and Jerry parted company, John had not had a hit in several years. John believed that he had been overexposed in the '70s, but I also know that Jerry had worked pretty hard to not overexpose his client. One example of this was when John first had a contract with ABC for a weekly John Denver television show to be fashioned like the popular musical variety shows featuring the Smothers Brothers and Glen Campbell.

It was Jerry who redirected John and ABC: Periodic television specials would be far better than a weekly television show. This was something that Jerry had also learned from Colonel Parker in his work with Elvis: People may not want to pay for concert tickets to see someone they can see for free on television every week. To this day, Elvis's '68 *Comeback Special* is seen and talked about. Would Elvis's performances on that special have had the power and interest if he had been on TV every week during those years? I doubt it.

Jerry died in 2015 at age 77. Although the two were never close again, they had cleared the air after their falling-out, and Jerry still deserves a lot of credit for the industry phenomenon that was John Denver.

Even in the absence of hits in his later years, John had amassed a fortune and still had significant income from publishing, performances, and CD sales. I don't know the particulars of his estate and how his inheritance was distributed, and frankly I wouldn't go into any detail even if I did. But I do know that in the end, all the kids were well taken care of. I can say that because I knew John and how important family was to him. Knowing that, it is still the biggest puzzle to me how a guy who made family his number one priority didn't have a will made out to provide for them. It got sorted out eventually, but not before some longtime relationships were strained to the point of breaking.

Part of John's show-day routine was always a long hot shower and shave as close to showtime as possible. Photo courtesy Lowell Norman.

Chapter 8

UNDER THE CIRCUS TENT

One of the most interesting aspects of working with a celebrity of John's stature was the access you have to that weird world of showbiz. Ever since circus trains have stopped in a town and set up their shows, people have lined up outside the tents (and now studios and stage back doors) waiting to get a glimpse of this mysterious world. We are fascinated by the personalities and how it all works.

I found it all intriguing when I first started working with John, but I also found that the romance wears off quickly.

There are two types of celebrity in my opinion: the *working class* and the *elite class*. The classification has nothing to do with popularity or where they stand in the showbiz community. It has to do with attitude.

The working class are people who just want to do their job the best they can and go home and live a normal life. They don't seek attention or press except whatever appropriate publicity or marketing they need to promote their product. They don't have paparazzi following them around or stage outings to build interest in their so-called brand. They just do their jobs. They have nothing to prove; they have already done that through their work. John Denver was definitely in the working class.

The elite class—well, let's just say they're the opposite.

Some of the nicest people I've met in show business were household names and had been around a long time. George Burns, Jay Leno, Lily Tomlin, to name a few. And some were up-and-comers fighting for a place on top—also nice people—like Debby Boone, Linda Ronstadt, and Karen Carpenter. But then some are as unpleasant as you can imagine. It's like anything in life, or any other business atmosphere. The same categories exist with those behind the scenes, by the way. Some are know-it-alls and act like they're celebrities because they work and hang around celebrities. Others are there to work their craft with as little fanfare as possible.

Behind those high studio walls that everyone wants to glance over is just a very diverse group of people whose business is showbiz. Nothing more. It's just a giant circus tent full of animals and clowns, acrobats and sword swallowers. In other words, it's a very fake world. Don't get me wrong, it's fun! But it's also fake.

Once you understand that, it's much easier to navigate without feeling intimidated. My initiation into this world was John's guest appearance with Bob Hope at NBC in Burbank in 1973. I had no business there other than to watch my new boss's segment being taped. He did a silly sketch with Hope, who was dressed up to look like John, and he sang a song with the band. This was also my introduction to John's manager, Jerry Weintraub. He was there with his entourage, as this was one of the first shows he booked for John on American television.

John did a lot of television those first few years after I came on board. He also, of course, starred in a major motion picture, *Oh, God!* There was a lot of John Denver activity in and around LA in the '70s, and most of his recording during that period was at RCA in Hollywood. I lived about an hour away, down the coast in Orange County, so anytime I wanted I could drive up and visit him on the set or in the studio. I always asked first, but I can't ever remember being refused, even though I usually had no official business there. This was before I was considered the de facto tour photographer. In fact, most often I wouldn't even bring a camera, as it would be a distraction. John understood my interest in all the aspects of production

On the set of *Rocky Mountain Christmas* with a very young Zak on his knee. Photo courtesy John Denver photo archive.

TOP: John and a golden eagle from a television special John did in the early '70s. Photo courtesy John Denver photo archive.

BOTTOM: John hosting *The Tonight Show* in the mid–'70s. From left: Dennis Weaver, Dick and Tommy Smothers, and George Gobel. Photo courtesy Lowell Norman.

TOP: John and Annie, Daisy, and Murphy. Shooting for the album cover *Back Home Again*. Photo courtesy Lowell Norman.

BOTTOM: The band and their families from the *Back Home Again* album shoot. Clockwise from left: Kris and Bonnie O'Connor with their girls, Darcy and Kelly, and their dog, Casey; Diane and Dick Kniss and their son, Jonathan; John's secretary, Peggy; Steve and Corline Weisberg; John Sommers; John and Annie Denver and their dogs Murphy and Daisy (cat names unknown). Photo courtesy Lowell Norman.

TOP: The band circa 1974–1976. From left: John Sommers, Dick Kniss, JD, Hal Blaine, and Steve Weisberg. Photo courtesy RCA Records.

BOTTOM: An odd match, but somehow they pulled it off. John with Frank Sinatra from a John Denver TV special. Photo courtesy Lowell Norman.

TOP: We spent a lot of free days playing softball while on tour. Here's John about to crush a line drive into left field. Photo courtesy Lowell Norman.

BOTTOM: Jay Leno played on our team when he opened for us at Harrah's Lake Tahoe. Photo courtesy Lowell Norman.

TOP: Lunch with Captain Cousteau and the crew of *Calypso*. Photo courtesy Cousteau Society.

BOTTOM: Our whale adventure found John and his diving crew on a catamaran following some humpback whales off the Kona coast in Hawaii. I spent most of our shooting days hanging out the door of our single engine Citabria waiting for some magic to happen. Photo courtesy Lowell Norman.

TOP: John's preshow ritual to get his voice ready: drinking hot tamari tea laced with a little whiskey. Note the Ping-Pong paddle tucked under his arm, Ping-Pong being another preshow ritual. Photo courtesy Lowell Norman.

BOTTOM: Rare shot of John with a beard. I took this photo in the Hollywood Hills while John was filming a public service commercial about recycling. He was way ahead of the curve on environmental issues. Photo courtesy Lowell Norman.

The author and his boss during the John Denver Celebrity Pro-Am Ski Tournament at Heavenly Valley, Lake Tahoe, mid-'80s. Photo courtesy Lowell Norman.

Backstage at Red Rocks. And because he's enjoying a beer, this shot had to be taken several hours before a concert. Photo courtesy Lowell Norman.

TOP AND BOTTOM: One of John's favorite places to be was in the pilot's seat of his Learjet 35. Photos courtesy Lowell Norman.

TOP: Fly fishing in the Roaring Fork River just south of Aspen and right outside the door of Barney Wyckoff's cabin off Independence Highway. Photo courtesy Lowell Norman.

BOTTOM: John doing some jumps for the camera on his Kawasaki. Photo courtesy Lowell Norman.

TOP LEFT: John and Cassandra. Photo courtesy John Denver photo archive.

TOP RIGHT: John and Annie. Photo courtesy John Denver photo archive.

BOTTOM: John and Joe Henry in John's study during a magazine interview about their song "Let Us Begin (What Are We Making Weapons For?)" Photo courtesy Lowell Norman.

TOP: My *I Want to Live* crew and more, at John's Aspen home after a shoot. Clockwise from left: Me, Mark Hanes, David Donnelly, Dorothy Duke, Steve Swear, Annie Denver, Keith Blume, Apollo astronaut Charlie Duke, and JD. Photo Courtesy Lowell Norman.

BOTTOM: John and a new friend at the Somalian refugee camp. Photo courtesy Werner Krutein.

TOP: A few special moments with Pope John Paul II outside the Vatican. Photo courtesy John Denver photo archive.

BOTTOM: John working out the chords to "Calypso" while onboard the *Calypso*. Photo courtesy Cousteau Society.

TOP: John in his element! Photo courtesy Lowell Norman.

BOTTOM: John in his element! Photo courtesy Edgar Boyles.

Windstar cofounder and tour security chief Tom Crum (left) with John at the Great Wall of China, 1980. Photo courtesy John Denver photo archive.

and freely offered to share his access with me whenever possible. He knew the more I was exposed to, the greater value I would be to his interests down the road.

I learned a lot by staying out of the way, just watching and listening. My ambition in life at that time was to be a film director. It was a logical ambition for someone who viewed the world through a photographic lens. I tended to frame everything around me in CinemaScope. Whatever was going on with the directors or producers intrigued me.

Television was (and to some extent still is) considered a producer's medium. Film is a director's medium. That becomes quite obvious when watching a television show being put together. The producer calls the shots, and TV directors are mostly relegated to the video truck switching what shots work best. In film, it's a much different world. Watching director Carl Reiner direct first-time film actor John Denver in *Oh, God!* was fascinating. John was a quick study and figured things out fast, but he still needed help on the little nuances of his character, whereas his costar, George Burns, just needed to be told Action and his instincts did the rest. Reiner was a seasoned director, always in control and never overbearing. He was curious, questioning, not afraid to seek answers to all the technical problems that arose during the filming. That was interesting to me, and was an important lesson to learn: to always question if you don't know how best to accomplish something, despite your title or position. The real pros never lose their inquisitiveness. I spent as many days as I could watching, always envisioning myself in that position as director.

I'll never forget hanging out with George Burns. Here was a guy who had seen it all, had been around show business for more than seventy years and was the most unassuming, gracious guy you can imagine. He was funny and engaging. When he showed up at Madison Square Garden on one of our concert nights, we had already met, and I was flattered that he remembered. We had flown in on the same 747 from LA, and I spent about an hour with him on one of those upstairs lounge couches that were available to first-class passengers in those days. The flight was not crowded so we pretty much had the lounge to ourselves. He was meeting John in New York for the first time ahead of shooting *Oh, God!* for Warner Bros. His long-time manager, Irving Fein, accompanied him. We talked about the shooting schedule and how this was only his second film in many years. So even with George, then in his late seventies, there was an inquisitiveness, a thirst for knowledge. He had his classic cigar in hand, unlit for the duration of the trip. I remember laughing a lot and listening to the way he told stories, and I realized that although his content was funny, it was his practiced presentation and timing that made me laugh.

We spent a few days hanging out on the movie set and at social gatherings in and around the making of the movie. A few years later, backstage at a concert in LA, I took a photo of John with George Burns and his new costar for the *Oh, God!* sequel, an eleven-year-old girl named Louanne Sirota. It was a passing of the baton. Louanne's character in *Oh, God! Book II* had the same kind of visitation from God that John had experienced in the original. It was basically the same storyline again, but it wasn't the box office hit that John and George had enjoyed.

John found the filmmaking process tedious. In the concert world, you show up, get dressed, go on stage, and do your thing. The prep and show are all done at your pace. With shooting a film, there was way too much waiting for the next scene. Hours could go by while they worked out the technical details. He was happy to be doing it but frustrated by the process. And in television and movies, he was working for someone else and frequently being someone else. John's music was a purely personal matter. They were his songs, his visions, his statements, his shows, his records, all adding to the persona he was. I think he enjoyed movies and television, but what he was able to express there was certainly muted compared to the music career that he had so carefully crafted as his own.

When we worked with Frank Sinatra on the television special John did with him, things were different. Sinatra would ask, "What time do you need me, and for how long?" If the answer was call time at 2 p.m. and we needed him for four hours, he was there at 2 p.m.—ready to go—and you had him till 6 p.m., and then he was gone, regardless of whether you were done. He was famous for this, and I got to see it firsthand. John and Frank and the orchestra had finished shooting a song together on a soundstage, and there was some technical glitch they had to work out. When they were ready to shoot again, the call came out, "Where's Francis? Anyone know where Mr. Sinatra is?" He was in a car and already miles away. It was 6:20 p.m.

Working with Sinatra in the back-to-back concerts we did at Harrah's Lake Tahoe in '75 and '76, he was much the same. His cocktail show followed our dinner show by about an hour and a half, and I would usually still be around when he went onstage. He would show up to dress about fifteen minutes before the show and would be gone immediately after. There was no hanging around backstage. You'd find him alone at a private baccarat table in the casino before all the guests even had time to leave the auditorium, his tuxedo tie loosely hanging around his collar, stiff drink at his side—exactly like you'd expect.

A lot had been made of Sinatra and the Rat Pack, and I'm sure those stories are mostly accurate, but I didn't see any of it. Perhaps those days were behind him.

To me, he seemed like a lonely guy. He'd show up to get ready for his gig alone, or silently enter the dressing area with his security guard. He'd stand backstage waiting for his cue alone, walk on stage from the curtains alone, and leave alone. I saw him many times in the casino there at Harrah's playing baccarat, always alone.

Maybe that's what made his *Only the Lonely* album one of the best records ever made—he lived it.

The one time I did get a hint of that former life of Sinatra's was the first time I saw him perform. Guitarist John Sommers and I went to the cocktail show and, because we were with the Denver entourage, they sat us at the front middle table. We were also the youngest guys in the audience, I'm sure. There were lots of suits sitting around us as I glanced at the others at our table of twelve.

I first noticed the comic Milton Berle and his wife. Next to her was Jack Benny's wife, who was sitting with our then recently disgraced ex-vice president Spiro Agnew and his wife. There were a couple of other older actresses there as well, but I don't recall who exactly they were. Sinatra's wife, Barbara (who had once been married to Zeppo Marx), was also sitting at our table. No card-carrying Rat Packers but still an impressive group of old-time showbiz personalities.

John Sommers and I sat among the shiny black tuxedos to enjoy the show and see what all the fuss was about this guy. I have to admit, I never really got Sinatra until that evening. His show was vintage Frank, and he had the audience from the second the spot hit him until curtain. By any measure, he was an amazing entertainer. I've often told people that they had no concept of John unless they saw him perform live. The same was true for Sinatra. I had no idea what a completely engaging entertainer he was until I saw him in person with the orchestra conducted by Count Basie.

During the '70s and into the '80s, John did a lot of television. Before the onslaught of hits, manager Jerry Weintraub had negotiated a weekly television show for John with ABC. When the hits were all of a sudden coming at a furious pace, he renegotiated John's television deal from a weekly show to a series of John Denver television specials. As I mentioned earlier, this was to mitigate his overexposure. It was a smart move on Jerry's part and a move that ensured John another ten years or more of concert success.

But it also posed a problem. How to continually fill those hour specials with interesting and entertaining content? At first, there was no problem with the Christmas special being the shining example of John doing television right. It was filled with songs and atmosphere, guest starred Olivia Newton-John, with lots of kids, family, and Christmas cheer. It was all shot in a field near Aspen in a transparent dome that looked like a soft, glowing snow globe. It was a magical television experience, as was his *An Evening with John Denver* special, which won him an Emmy Award for Outstanding Special—Comedy-Variety or Music in 1975.

For me, that was exactly how you packaged and sold John on television—feature his popular songs plus classic tunes sung with guests who complemented his vocal style and personality. Unfortunately, that quality did not translate to all his television performances. I may be alone in this criticism, but I thought the majority of television that John made was silly. It created an image of him that was not serious and tried to make a song-and-dance guy out of a guy who couldn't dance and really didn't want to. For millions, he went from a serious folk singer with a great voice and social conscience to a clown. In fact, I think this television image scared off his core audience of socially minded college students and young professionals.

You could argue, as Jerry did, that his television specials expanded his audience, but I think it also weakened it, made it less potent as a collective force for change. I like using the Bob Dylan example (an artist who was also managed by Jerry Weintraub). Dylan, like John, was a poet of song. The only real difference between them was their approach. Dylan didn't have any interest in anything but the music and the message. And neither did John. But unlike Dylan, who was completely comfortable just being himself on stage, John hid his insecurity as a musician behind a somewhat giddy, aw-shucks persona, as encouraged by Jerry. Not fake but definitely played up for the audience, and especially magnified for the television audience, a personal strategy of his that had begun evolving back in his Mitchell Trio days as the fun one in the group.

When you don't take yourself seriously at every level, how can you expect others to take you seriously? This is why there was never a love affair between John and the music critics. I used to read all our reviews as we traveled from city to city, hoping to get a glimpse of my name or an acknowledgment of the visual part of the show. I often did, but what I really remember is how the negative criticism of John was almost unanimous. Words like *sweet* and *saccharine* were used extensively, almost as if all the critics had gotten together and penned an anti-Denver manifesto. I know that these reviews, more often than not, were largely influenced by John's television exposure and not his talent as an artist, songwriter, and singer. John read them too, of course, and I believe it hurt him much more than he let on.

Not to be left out, that snobby derision came at John from his fellow musicians, too. Country music purists could be just as cutting as the music press, having never accepted John's music as authentic country, whatever that means. In 1975, John was nominated for Entertainer of the Year by the Country Music Association Awards. At the televised ceremony, the previous year's winner, Charlie Rich, opened the envelope with the winner's name. When he saw that it was John Denver, he pulled out his lighter and set fire to the card before announcing John's name. John graciously accepted his award via satellite, as we were touring in Australia, and he was wholly unaware at the time of the disrespectful gesture.

John would have been just as gracious if he had known. He was who he was, and he wasn't going to change, even if he had his own internal battles going on when trying to find his place. Most times, John ignored his critics and lived his life his way. But deep inside, he wanted to be acknowledged, he needed to be accepted. Interestingly, his loyal fan base remained just that—loyal.

During the television years, I was fortunate to meet and work with some really talented people. Not just those in front of the camera, but behind the scenes, too. One performer who impressed me a great deal was Karen Carpenter. She received the same saccharine slams from reviewers her whole life. But she was the real deal, from where I sat.

My involvement with Karen and Richard Carpenter was brief. John did a guest appearance on their television special, a favor for their new manager—who else? Jerry Weintraub—and they wanted to use some of my film footage of John climbing a mountain as a backdrop to one of his songs, which worked great. I got to sit through rehearsals and get a glimpse of how that Carpenters sound was made. Karen had one of the greatest female voices in pop music, in my estimation.

And yes, she really could play the drums! And did so in concerts. But playing the drums live is very different from recording drum parts for an album. This she left to my pal Hal Blaine, who you hear as drummer on most of their recordings.

Another celebrity I met was figure skater Dorothy Hamill, right after the Winter Olympics that made her famous. John was performing at Madison Square Garden, and Jane Weintraub asked me to accompany Dorothy to her seat and stay with her until the show started, which I happily did. Jerry Weintraub had just signed on as Dorothy's manager, and we talked about the sponsorship deal he got her for eyeglasses and what a big payday it was. I ended up watching the first half of the show with her but never saw her again.

On the Denver television special called *John Denver and The Ladies*, John featured a bevy of female singers, among them the Queen of Rock and

Roll, the one and only Tina Turner. Now there's a presence you cannot deny. There was nothing saccharine about Tina Turner. When she entered the room, you knew it. She was a huge talent in a tightly wound package. When she did the special with John, she was in her late thirties, and you'd never know it. Amazing energy.

There were some more magical moments hanging around those television tapings, and I was privileged to witness how they all went down. John got along with everybody and enjoyed working with other entertainers, and I know they all felt the same about him and his talent, regardless of how the press had demeaned him. Olivia Newton-John told us of John's personal hospitality that came from their work together on the song "Fly Away" and on the *Rocky Mountain Christmas* television special. "He was just a lovely, open, sweet man, and very warm to me," Olivia said. "I remember that I had my first snowy Thanksgiving at their house, and it was a very special day for me to be invited. It was when he was married to Annie, whom I loved. We were doing a Christmas special in Aspen, and Valerie Harper and Steve Martin and a number of wonderful guests were there. That was a special memory, and then he invited me to sing "Fly Away." I hadn't been [in America] very long, and I remember going to the studio, and there was an orchestra, and his producer [Milt Okun] was there. That was a big deal for me, to be singing with someone like him. He holds a special place in my heart."

After Olivia Newton-John died in August 2022, my thoughts went back to the time when I met her. It was a warm summer evening in either '75 or '76, and we were in the first of a two-week stand at Harrah's Lake Tahoe.

Backstage was buzzing because Olivia and her then manager and partner Lee Kramer were spotted in John's dressing room.

After the shows at Harrah's, there was always a little impromptu reception in the dressing area, a time for the musicians and guests to meet and relax. I was mingling as usual and happened to mention to Annie Denver that I had a crush on Olivia. (We all did, by the way.)

In classic Annie style, she took me by the shirtsleeve and presented me to Olivia. "Olivia, this is a friend of ours, Lowell Norman. He does all the visuals you saw in the show tonight." And with that, Annie turned to talk to another guest, leaving me and Olivia there alone.

Knowing I would now have to strike up a conversation with Olivia, and a little nervous about that, I almost faltered, but to my surprise and delight, she immediately had questions for me. The visuals had scenes of the Rockies and many of the animals found there, like the bighorn sheep, deer, bears, and such. She had a million questions about how I shot and assembled it to match the tunes in the show (remember, music videos were still five or six years away).

We had a very pleasant fifteen minutes together, and her excitement for what I had put together for the show was more than gratifying. Our paths never crossed again, but for those few minutes she made me feel like I was her new best friend. The week Olivia passed, I sent Annie a text thanking her for that memory. Annie's response was, in part, "That's beautiful Lowell . . . Olivia was so courageous . . . John and I both had a crush on her, I think everyone did." (See, I told you!) Olivia *was* courageous. She fought off cancer for over a decade, eventually losing that battle but not before bringing both awareness and clinical options to women fighting the same fight. A real hero and the sweetest, most sincere celebrity I had the pleasure to know, if only for a few minutes.

Years later, the shows that are more firmly and permanently embedded in my memory are two of the five hosting gigs John did at the Grammy Awards. My wife, Deb and I had recently gotten married, and John invited us to attend. I figured we'd sit somewhere behind all the singers and bands, but they sat us up front and center, right behind Sting and the Police. The memorable part of that show for me was what was going on backstage. Here were, all in one place at one time, the industry's best and brightest, with some of the biggest egos imaginable, somehow all getting along and hitting their marks when they needed to. It was a well-oiled machine, and the smoothness of it all was really a testament to producer Pierre Cossette's leadership.

Part of our attendance included the big, official Grammy after-party, which was normally a ten-minute drive to a downtown LA hotel, but it took us an hour to get through the traffic and park. Deb got to meet one of her favorites, soul singer Lou Rawls. He was friendly, and they spoke for some time. For her, that made the night. But the party itself was a bust. Almost all the big names threw their own parties or their record companies put them on. Some made a quick appearance and then went to other waiting parties.

That's the other thing about showbiz you get over pretty quickly: the buzz. The anticipation of something that never really pans out in quite the way you had originally thought it would. The Grammy after-party is a perfect example. The buzz was that you'd get up close and personal with the evening's performers and Grammy winners, sipping drinks from the open bar and eating hors d'oeuvres alongside your musical heroes.

Nope. Doesn't work like that. The party is full of industry execs and friends of industry execs, and friends of friends of industry execs, all congratulating each other with one eye scanning the ballroom to see what celebrity may have arrived. Deb and I thought, "This is it?" After half an hour, we went home.

The showbiz aspect of John's career and my time working with him is the least meaningful to me, and I think most everyone who has navigated that world at some level feels the same. It lacks the human element and creativity that the rest of John's world had. Would I trade my experiences and opportunities? Never. The circus that is show business is a fun place to be for sure. John and I and everyone in the organization had fun doing it. Just don't ever take it too seriously. It will leave you empty.

John knew this all too well. It's why he always had a certain disdain for Los Angeles, and he often grumbled about the amount of time he had to spend there. And it's also why he didn't have a lot of close personal relationships with other famous celebrities. It was a long way from the Rockies.

Herb Pedersen, Denny Brooks, and John singing "Wake Up Little Susie" at sound check, Red Rocks.
Photo courtesy Lowell Norman.

Chapter 9

BANDS OF BROTHERS

Although John did his fair share of solo concerts, or what he referred to as his one-man show, he loved playing concerts with his band. There was a chemistry with his musicians that was obvious to the audience—a mutual respect and close-knit bond that only musicians understand. I believe this is why, in the twenty-four years I was around each band configuration, there was never any disharmony or petty disagreements among them. That, and the fact that John did not scrimp on his band in any way, afforded him the best and most professional musicians available. John loved his band members, and I believe the admiration was shared by each of them too.

In the three decades I worked with John, there were three different bands. And they pretty much coincided with the decades. When I first traveled with John, there were only two sidemen in his band: Steve Weisberg and Dick Kniss. Just a few months before I arrived, Steve took over lead guitar from Mike Taylor, whose picture you see on the *Rocky Mountain High* album with Dick Kniss and Kris O'Connor.

I'm going to break it down here, beginning with that first band. Note that the '80s band really was formed in the late '70s, and members came and went, irrespective of the date. For clarity, I've used the decades to identify the bands.

The '70s Band

Dick Kniss (Bass)

In the beginning, the band definitely had a folk sound. Dick played upright base with John from the early '70s into the '80s. Dick was the fourth (and unseen) member of the folk trio Peter, Paul and Mary throughout the '60s. In old newsreel footage, you can spot him positioned behind the trio—usually in the shadow of the spotlight with his upright base in hand. When the trio disbanded for a time, and each went on to do their own solo work, John commandeered Dick to play for him.

Dick lived in Queens with his wife, Diane. A New York jazz musician at heart, he played gigs with local jazz bands throughout his career with JD. He was always the oldest guy on the road with us, being in his mid-thirties when I first met him in 1973. To me, he was the old sage of the group, and because I asked a lot of questions as I marched through life, and because he was always patient and receptive to my constant curiosities, I learned a lot from him about how to conduct myself and navigate life on the road. He was a sweet and gentle soul, and to everyone on the tour, he was known as Uncle Dick. I really can't remember him ever raising his voice or ever being anything but chill.

Best of all, of course, he was a solid bass player. He traveled with an enormous upright bass, for which the tour purchased an airline ticket because he refused to let it be trucked from concert to concert with all the sound gear. Although the instrument was bigger than Dick, he dragged it through countless airline terminals and jockeyed it into its seat on countless commercial flights. When we began to fly our own chartered planes, it found a resting place in the aisle or in the back lavatory.

Dick was a constant on the tour and played on all of John's recordings through the '70s and into the '80s. He's also credited as one of the writers of "Sunshine on My Shoulders." When he parted company with John in 1978, he was in his forties and his time on the road with John was over. By then Peter, Paul and Mary had started a reunion tour. Dick once again became their bassist and appeared with them until Mary Travers's death in 2009. He made his final appearance with Peter Yarrow and Noel (Paul) Stookey in December of that year.

Dick died on January 25, 2012, in Saugerties, New York, at age seventy-four.

Steve Weisberg (Guitar, Dobro, Pedal Steel)

Steve's story of first working with John is similar to my own—except he looked to lend fate a hand by actually moving from his hometown of Dallas, Texas, to Aspen with the intention of being discovered by John. His reasoning was that it was a small community, which it was in 1973, and if he hung out in the right spots, he would eventually run into him. It worked. He was asked to audition in early '73, and after three different auditions, he won the spot to replace Mike Taylor. Steve played a Taylor six string, and on 'Berkeley Woman' played dulcimer. Later he would add a pedal steel guitar on John's more country-oriented tracks.

Steve was known to us all as "Pokey," a name Kris O'Connor first called him because he was the most easily sidetracked traveler—a trait KO, who was responsible for our staying on schedule, couldn't stand. Steve was a funny and personable guy who was always happy and easy to like. He was born to be on stage and loved the attention.

Surprisingly, he lasted fewer than five full years with John. I think his departure was a huge blow for him, and it wasn't too long after that he divorced his first wife and relocated back to Dallas, where he eventually went back to his family's roots and got into the apparel business. We stayed in touch for some time, and he was helpful to me in my effort to produce an Internet startup. But in his spare time, he was busy lending his considerable talent to local Texas bands.

After John died in '97, Steve was a regular at the Aspen JD reunion gigs held each year on the anniversary of John's death. After a fight with cancer, Steve passed away in May 2014 at age sixty-four.

John Martin Sommers (Guitar, Banjo, Mandolin, Fiddle)

In the fall of 1973, a country swing band from Aspen named Liberty joined us to open a couple of shows in the Northwest. One of their founding members was musician, singer, and songwriter John Sommers. Sommers had written "Thank God I'm a Country Boy." John Denver saw them perform it on stage at a club in Snowmass and told them he wanted to record it. In many ways the group was a perfect fit as an opening act for John: an energetic and tight band that played a lot of original tunes along with some esoteric country swing and bluegrass songs.

But when we went out on the road again, the very next week, Sommers went from being in the opening act to joining the main attraction as he became a part of the band. He brought along with his backup vocals a Martin six-string guitar, banjo, mandolin, and fiddle. The band was now three members and growing.

Sommers fit in beautifully with the band and his addition produced a much bigger and more diverse sound. He traveled with us during the glory years, when John was the biggest record-selling artist of the decade.

When John decided he was going to shake up the band in 1977, Sommers was the only one he decided to keep on. The first order of business with the new band would be recording the album I Want to Live. The second day of recording, Sommers took John aside and told him he couldn't do it. The new members of the band were just too intimidating, and he felt he couldn't keep up. It sounds crazy, but that's how a lot of musicians respond to the pressures of recording.

At the same time, you had to understand that Sommers found himself suddenly in a band with mostly ex-Elvis alums. These guys were the best of the best: James Burton, Glen D. Hardin, and Jerry Scheff. After Elvis's death in '77, these guys were suddenly available and John grabbed them before anyone else could, thanks in part to the relationship that had been honed between Elvis's people and Jerry Weintraub.

In the end, Sommers left the band. A year or two later John invited him to sit in with the band when they did a couple shows in Texas. I was not there to witness it, but as John tells it in his book, and how I heard it from others who were there, Sommers had a sudden impulse that he should be the leader of this band. It was a long and loud meeting that followed, and it would be the last meeting they would ever have together.

Sad on many levels, including the fact that Sommers, an ex-navy pilot, was a good friend of John's for many years, and had been with the band for eight years.

Sommers went back to his love—writing songs and performing in small clubs in and around his home in Aspen. He eventually moved west to try his hand at being a studio musician.

Hal Blaine (Percussion, Drums)

Soon after John Sommers joined the band, Hal Blaine began touring with us. For me, this was a momentous move. I had been a huge fan of Hal Blaine's for years, without even knowing his name. He was the drums and percussion on virtually every important album I owned as a teenager; he played for the Mamas and the Papas, the Beach Boys, the Byrds, Simon & Garfunkel, and dozens more. He was the guy I imitated with my drumsticks as I listened for hours to my LPs.

Hal was an institution in the recording business, a founding member of the famous Wrecking Crew, the group of studio musicians everyone—and I mean *everyone*—hired to create their hits. In his home in the Hollywood Hills, he had an entire living room and hallway filled with gold and platinum albums for his years of session work. He was part of the famous Wall of Sound developed by legendary record producer Phil Spector. He knew everybody, had worked with everybody, had been everywhere, and he was the most modest, engaging, and funny guy I had ever met. He had a deep, throaty voice, a slight Boston accent, and commanding presence. He was forty-five when I first met him, so he took Dick Kniss's place as the old man of the band.

When first starting with John, he came with only his percussion setup. A drum kit would be added later. Hal became a valued friend to me and was often my seating partner on our frequent long flights. Once we arrived at our hotel, you wouldn't see Hal again until we were boarding our transportation to the venue. No matter where we were in the world, Hal had been there and done that. He preferred the hermit's life on tour, and it took a lot to get him out of his room and to see the sights on off days.

Hal loved John and really took a loss leaving session work behind to tour with him. As a studio drummer, you are paid by the session, and if you worked it like Hal did, you could make a very good living, which Hal had done for years. But going on the road with John was special, and it represented the pinnacle of touring in those days; the steady work it offered and the kick of playing before a live audience were worth the sacrifice.

Hal's last tour with John was our 1980 tour of Japan. He continued to do session work well into his seventies on other projects and with other recording artists. In 1990, he published his book *Hal Blaine and the Wrecking Crew*. I visited him after he moved to Palm Desert. Although he had slowed down, he was still on the phone accepting recording dates and looking forward to hanging out with his session musician friends.

Hal passed away at the age of ninety on March 11, 2019, in Palm Desert.

The '80s Band

Herb Pedersen (Guitar, Banjo)

Herb joined the band as part of the new sound John was looking for and to replace Steve Weisberg. Herb was a serious musician, but when he was not on stage or practicing for hours in his hotel room, he was one of the most fun guys to hang with. We were both early risers and most days on the road we often ate breakfast together before any of the others had opened their eyes. While touring Europe, if the opportunity arose we would rent a car and visit somewhere we had pegged as a place we wanted to see. The bus or transportation we took to get to the evening's concert venue usually left the hotel around 4 or 5 p.m., giving us most of the day to explore.

Herb was much more than a sideman. He was a writer, producer, and performer in his own right, and he had made several solo albums by the time he began his stint with John. Herb was perhaps the most vocal about what he felt was John's complacency regarding his music. He felt he was too distracted by all the other extracurricular activities John had going on in his life and felt he needed to get serious about his music instead of coasting through on his former hits. He knew there was a lot more music in him. As carefree and fun as he was, when it came to music and the band, Herb was strictly business and took his craft seriously. I can say that of all the musicians I've been around, he was the most disciplined.

Herb's tenure with John lasted only four years. Later, Herb went on to help start the Desert Rose Band with his friend Chris Hillman of the Byrds and fronted his own band, the Laurel Canyon Ramblers. As of this writing, at seventy-six years young, he and Chris continue to work together with no signs of slowing down.

James Burton (Guitar, Dobro)

As the leader of Elvis Presley's famous TCB Band, James Burton ushered in a whole new sound to the Denver band, bringing with him TCB Band alums Glen D. Hardin on keyboards and Jerry Scheff on bass. The stage was getting crowded.

James was already a legend by the time he started with John. His big break came in the mid-1950s when he got a call to meet a young Ricky Nelson, who wanted to start a band of his own to add more appeal to his family's TV show, *The Adventures of Ozzie and Harriet*. James was still in his teens but had a successful career locally with performers from his hometown of Shreveport, Louisiana. He had already recorded the rock and roll standard "Susie Q" with Dale Hawkins. The Nelsons were impressed with the talent and Southern demeanor of young James. They not only asked him to join the Ricky Nelson band, but they also invited him to stay in their home while working with Ricky. He stayed there for two years.

While working for Nelson, James had time to do recording sessions in LA and became a member of the famous Wrecking Crew, a group of highly sought-after session players who, in the late '50s and '60s, were the musicians you heard on nearly every hit record of the era.

From James's website comes this explanation of how he started with Elvis: "In 1968, James got the call from Elvis Presley to be on his comeback television special, but at the time he was working with Frank Sinatra and unavailable. Elvis told James how he always watched the *Ozzie and Harriet* show just to see him play. It was no surprise that when Elvis called James back in '69 to start up a band for his Las Vegas engagement, he was there. It was a very tough decision to make, since his studio career was very busy and very lucrative. Burton had already turned down an offer by Bob Dylan to go on tour. Sessions were usually booked three months in advance, so Presley gave Burton a few months to get the band together."

The rest is history, as they say. James would remain with Elvis until Elvis's untimely death in 1977. Shortly after, he began his fifteen-year stint with John Denver.

In March 2001, James was inducted into the Rock & Roll Hall of Fame. Keith Richards, Rolling Stones guitarist and longtime Burton fan, was part of the ceremonies, telling attendees, "I never bought a Ricky Nelson record; I bought a James Burton record."

Jim Horn (Saxophone, Flute)

Jim Horn was another member of the Wrecking Crew. He played just about any reed instrument there was, but with John he mostly played tenor, baritone, and bass saxophone, and flute. I first met Jim when John was recording the *I Want to Live* album. I was about to start editing our hunger documentary of the same title and needed some bumper segues to make the editing work. So, John had Jim do all sorts of little segues, just a few bars each, from the chorus of the title track of *I Want to Live*. It worked well and made sense, as the film ended with that song and the music video I had put together for it.

Like Hal and Herb and James, Jim was already a legend in the business. He had worked with all the best, including Mick Jagger, Emmylou Harris, the Beach Boys, and Duane Eddy. He agreed to do a tour with John after they recorded that album and ended up a fixture onstage until John's untimely death.

Jim relocated from the Northwest to Nashville and continued his session work playing on hit records by Garth Brooks, Kenny Chesney, Wynonna, and Blake Shelton.

Jerry Scheff (Bass)

Jerry was another TCB Band member who toured with Elvis until his death. John offered him a spot in the band at the same time he hired the other TCB Band members, James Burton and Glen D. Hardin. Jerry's big break came in the '60s when, as a session musician, he played the bass part on "Along Comes Mary," a hit by vocal group the Association. In the following years, he worked for the Everly Brothers, Nancy Sinatra, Johnny Rivers, Neil Diamond, Sammy Davis Jr., Johnny Mathis, and the Nitty Gritty Dirt Band, among others. In 1971, Scheff recorded bass parts for the Doors' *L.A. Woman* album, including his distinctly recognizable contribution to the hit song "Riders on the Storm."

Later, Jerry would work with Bob Dylan on the acclaimed album *Street-Legal*, in addition to session work with Johnny Cash. In the '80s, he toured with both John and Elvis Costello.

In mid-1985, Jerry's twenty-three-year-old son, Jason, joined the band Chicago, after Peter Cetera departed.

Emory Gordy Jr. (Bass)

Another Elvis alum, Emory Gordy Jr., joined the Denver band in 1979. Earlier, along with fellow TCB Band members James Burton and Glen D. Hardin, he accompanied Gram Parsons and Emmylou Harris on Parson's *Grievous Angel* album, released the year after Parsons's untimely death in 1973.

In the mid-1970s, he was an original member of Emmylou Harris's Hot Band along with James Burton, Glen D. Hardin, John Ware, Rodney Crowell, and Hank DeVito. Remaining with Harris until 1977, Gordy continued to get calls from LA studios, where he played bass on projects by the Bellamy Brothers, Billy Joel, and Tom Petty. By 1979, he had joined John's band, touring the United States, Australia, and Europe with us, and he later composed the bass tracks for two of John's albums.

Dan Wheetman (Guitar, Fiddle)

Dan was one of the original members of the Aspen band Liberty that opened for John during the 1975 tour. His deep baritone voice and talented fiddle playing led John to hire him as a background vocalist and musician in '78.

He remained a fixture on tour until John's death. Today Wheetman is a member of the bluegrass band Marley's Ghost and has created two musical productions for stage, including *Mark Twain's River of Song* and *The Road: My Life with John Denver*.

Denny Brooks (Guitar)

Back in the mid-1960s, a young, new solo performer named John Denver opened for Denny Brooks, who at the time had a promising solo career. The two got along and kept a friendship that would eventually come full circle when Denny joined the band from '76 until '86 as a background vocalist.

Brooks was a frequent opening act for singer-songwriter Hoyt Axton. Denny sings the beautiful and moving country song "San Antone" on the soundtracks to the films *Rolling Thunder* and *The Ninth Configuration*. In addition, he has also sung on the soundtracks for the western *Mustang Country* and the Chuck Norris action vehicle *Breaker! Breaker!* Denny does a musical tribute retrospective on John called *John Denver: A Friend Remembers* and has sung in *Back Home Again: A John Denver Holiday Concert*, which has toured all over the United States.

Denny died in July 2018.

The '90s Band

John took some time off from concert performances in the late '80s. By the early '90s, when he decided to give it a go again, he had formed a new band, mostly made up of Nashville session musicians. This was mostly an acoustic setup, and John performed now in smaller, more intimate venues. Frequently joining this new band were Denver band alums James Burton, Glen D. Hardin (piano), Jim Horn, and Dan Wheetman. The '90s band that played with John until his death were Chris Nole (piano, synthesizer, and vocals), Pete Huttlinger (guitars, banjo, mandolin, and vocals), Alan Deremo (electric bass guitar), and Michito Sanchez (percussion and drums).

People might think of the musicians who back up a lead singer as faceless technicians, but nothing could be further from the truth. These talented artists played a vital role on the stage and in the studio. Some have passed, some have moved on, but all had a huge part in bringing the music of John Denver to life.

John doing a little spring skiing somewhere in Colorado. Photo courtesy John Denver photo archive.

Chapter 10

STARWOOD IN ASPEN

If you follow the Roaring Fork River up-valley from Glenwood Springs, past Carbondale and Basalt, and up to the Aspen airport, look east up at the hills and you'll get a glimpse of what was the Denver property on Johnson Drive in an area known as Starwood. That view is as close as you would get unless you were an invited guest or could talk your way past the armed guard at the gate a half mile down the hill.

When I first visited in '73, there was no guarded gate, let alone an armed gatekeeper. But as development in the area continued, and an alarming number of uninvited guests began to wander onto the property, John got permission to construct a gatehouse at the entrance to Starwood that not only served to increase his security, but also that of the other residents in this exclusive area.

Moving past the security house and rounding a mile-long semiloop, you would come to John and Annie Denver's house. From the road you'd only see the rooftop, as the property was built into a gentle slope. The home I first visited in '73 was not particularly big or pretentious. Designed by John and a local architect, it was essentially a three-bedroom, two-bath home of about 3,200 square feet. Built on levels in the shed style, the main, or entrance, level contained the kitchen and dining room, and to the far north, the primary suite. Below was the formal living room, although nothing about the house was formal in a stuffy sense.

Bright and cheerful, Annie's decorating was as warm and inviting as it was mountain chic. Sitting at an elevation of 7,000 feet, the setting was chilly in the shade and evening, and warm and bright in the daylight sun. There was a small pool outside the kitchen door (later a spa was added). A few steps up from the main level was a guest room and bath, and above that was a long landing that also served as the library. A four-step ladder took you to a loft with a bed and a skylight overhead, and a step or two beyond that was a small roof patio. Sometime near the end of the '70s, that outdoor roof patio served as a platform for an amazing telescope. It was a gift from the widow of Wernher von Braun, the famous and somewhat controversial father of modern rocketry. Wernher had been a sort of hero to John long before they actually met, and the two became friends while John was helping promote NASA and its civilians-in-space program.

The house was built to be open and airy. From level three you could clearly hear everything that was going on in level one. The door to the primary suite and the door to the one guest room and bathroom were really the only doors in the place. It probably wasn't the intention, but the house as built was a perfect party house—it was intimate and open at the same time, and there was plenty of room to entertain. The large windows throughout, along with aspen trees and scrub oak surrounding the house with a view of the valley and Capitol Peak beyond, made you feel at home there in the Rocky Mountains. Even in a winter storm.

One of my first memories of my time there was when I was stranded for a couple of days. On the day I was to leave for home, the Aspen airport shut down, and a snowstorm blew through. As it began to clear, John and Annie decided to stick with their plans to cross-country ski to a cabin where some friends were meeting for an overnight stay. They'd just bring me along.

Which was fine, but I'd never cross-country skied before, and didn't have any gear, including a decent jacket for the cold. So, on our way John stopped at a ski store, rented me some skis, got them all waxed properly, and then—right there in the parking lot—taught me how to use them. (Although he offered, I didn't let him buy me a ski jacket—a decision I soon came to regret.)

Off we went. I picked up the skill well enough to keep up with them as we ascended the snow trail. About twenty minutes into this endeavor, we met two of the gang we were going to stay with coming down. One guy's beard was a giant icicle. "Don't even try to go up," they insisted. "The rest of them are on their way down. It's cold, windy, and too dangerous." I was thrilled with this news as I was already shivering in my poorly insulated coat. An hour later, we were all toasty warm at John's house. We had an impromptu party that afternoon and, later, a meal in Aspen. I flew home the next afternoon when the airport opened.

I had taken at least a couple rolls of film on my first stay there back in '73, but time and several moves have unfortunately left me without them. It's too bad, as the original house was something special. Later, as John's family grew, so did the house, with the addition of several more bedrooms and baths, a music studio, a larger living room, and an expanded kitchen. The original layout became swallowed up in the monstrous additions. With this newly expanded floor plan, the house lost the quaintness and personality of a mountain getaway and now resembled more of a rock star's mountain estate.

Still, it was a warm and inviting place to be. Annie made certain of that. It's hard to describe the influence she had on creating the welcoming atmosphere you felt when visiting the Denvers. The warmth and joy there in the years she made it her home was palpable. I felt the contrast years later, when John was living there alone, the moment I walked through the door. Missing was the laughter and warmth Annie brought into that space. The smell of home cooking and the robust activity of family life were gone. The spirit that had lived there and made that house a home was now a mile down the road, in a new house of her own design.

It makes one wonder how much of those years of constant building and adding on was really just a distraction from the intense marital problems John and Annie were facing. The pressures and temptations of celebrity, the increasing number of days away from home, Annie's increased interest in cultivating her own circle of friends, and John's constant guilt for not making quality time with his kids all contributed to the failing marriage. When all the building stopped and the house was ready to be enjoyed, the joy in the marriage seemed gone.

Down a sixty-yard path from the house was the guesthouse and office. Although never really used then as an office, the outbuilding did house a large brass-framed pyramid that John sat under to meditate. The guesthouse was a long, straight structure built into the property's slope. It had three bedrooms and two baths, a projection-theater setup, a small kitchen, and a primary suite. One entire side of the structure was glass with a jaw-dropping western panoramic view of the valley and peaks beyond.

A dirt road took you down to the guesthouse from the main house. The Denvers had several four-wheel drive vehicles and always made one available to me while I was there. All the outbuildings on the property were constructed so they could make the most out of passive solar technology. There was a lot of glass to let in the warmth of the sun and lots of mass to contain or store that heat. My experience was that the still nascent technology wasn't always reliable, especially in the winter months, so, thankfully, there was conventional heating too.

Part of the main house, after the large expansion, was designed to be a sort of solar energy demonstration lab. One small room off the bedroom additions had a computer that was tasked with monitoring and tracking the temperatures of the rooms during the day. John saw the house as a sort of living organism and his attention to documenting its energy usage was indeed prescient. Although, in reality, the computer documentation of the building's energy consumption didn't last long. Either no one had the time to keep it up, or interest in it waned.

Sometimes John would summon me to Aspen to take care of some project, such as a video to be used in a concert, or sometimes just to organize his unruly and growing photography library. On those trips I would usually stay in the guesthouse and was happy to do so, particularly as tensions grew between Annie and John. Still, I rarely saw any strife between the two of them. And there were times I stayed at the guesthouse and never saw John and maybe saw Annie only once. Nevertheless, Annie always made me feel welcome.

For instance, I arrived once with a bad cold to stay in the guesthouse. Annie asked me to write down what I needed for the next couple of days. I made the list and left it near the kitchen sink, figuring I'd be visited by a delivery boy or one of the hired help. But no, later in the day Annie walked into the guesthouse kitchen with a grocery bag full of food and meds for me. She had gone to the store and picked them up herself. That was Annie.

The one feature of the expanded main house that was really special was the kitchen. It sported a large teppanyaki range built into an island in the middle of the floor, an expression of John's expanding interest in an alternative diet.

He had an interesting relationship with food. In my early years of traveling with the band, we were pretty much on our own for breakfast and lunch but gathered together for a big evening meal after the concert, usually at a local restaurant John knew of or the local promoter arranged for us. In those first years when we traveled light, there were usually just ten or twelve of us for dinner. We'd enjoy a steak when in Kansas City, Mexican food in Tucson, crawdads in the South, and lobster in the Northeast. My favorite tour location was New York City because there were so many great opportunities to sample different cuisines.

By the beginning of 1980, however, John's body was telling him to slow down on all meat and rich food. He was starting to feel lethargic on tour and lacked the energy he had when he was younger. He also bought into all kinds of food fads at the time, making it even more of a trial in finding something he could eat. We would still dine out, but John would order light: a baked potato or rice and vegetables. The next natural step in his quest to eat smarter was bringing along with him on tour a personal chef. The first one was a character by the name of Ron Lemire.

Ron was a low-key, ex-merchant marine officer and Golden Gloves boxer. His official job title was chief of security, but that was to stroke his ego. Ron was, in truth, John's cook and assistant. His idea of tour security was to walk through the venue before the show started and report back to John what *aura* he felt (a New Age reference to *atmosphere* or *energy*). If Ron felt the *aura* was a friendly blue, as he most always did, then he said it was a safe crowd and John could perform. This comforted John to some extent. A red aura would have been very dangerous, although, from a practical point of view, it meant very little as to whether John performed. Later, after a couple of scares happened following the aura method, John hired an actual professional security man named Bill McGilvry who had a different method of operation. Bill tucked a .357 Magnum in his boot, and, if he didn't like the look of someone, he was on them like a cheap suit until they proved themselves not to be a threat.

With Ron now out of the security business, he could concentrate on what his real job was: cooking for John. Under his care, John began to embrace a strict macrobiotic diet. Here's the way it worked on the road: Ron would set up shop in John's hotel suite with a load of pots and pans, a Coleman three-burner stove, and boxes of packaged rice, miso, and condiments. He whipped up some amazing meals. Once at a posh hotel located in Lake Geneva, Wisconsin (at one time a Playboy club), Ron went "shopping" with a shovel for some local herbs on the hotel grounds. He later returned with a large burdock root, which the personal chef dragged through the lobby to the elevator and up to John's room. No one stopped him or asked any questions, almost as if it were a normal occurrence. This was Ron's level of commitment to finding fresh local ingredients.

John was so knocked out by the Ron Diet that he told Annie that she needed to start cooking like his road chef. Big mistake. Annie was a great cook in her own right, and I think that directive did not sit well at all. Ron had to deal with Annie's wrath for years after that, not so much aimed at him but more at John for his less-than-diplomatic request.

Ron was way ahead of the curve in the nutrition craze. After he left touring with John, he became well known as a movement trainer for professional athletes. He also invented the LiquidTrainer, a breakthrough biofeedback device.

John used to say in concert that he tried to maintain a vegetarian diet but that it was hard to pass up a good taco. That always made me laugh, although it was really true. He would mix the discipline of his vegetarian diet with frequent indulgences and have a steak, or yes, a taco.

After the divorce from Annie in 1982, John had several road companions who would look out for his interests and help out when he had the kids, who were still less than ten years old at the time of the divorce. Roger Floyd was one, and later a guy by the name of Malcolm McDonald. I suppose their official job description was security detail, but in truth they functioned more as personal secretaries and valets. Both of these guys were great friends of John's and easy to be around. Malcolm (who John referred to in his autobiography as a true medicine man) was with John up until the very end, and I'm told he was one of the people who helped identify John's remains.

During their adolescent years and later, John's kids, Anna Kate and Zak, would occasionally show up on the road with John, usually with a nanny and John's assistants. This was supposed to be time with their dad, I'm sure, but the rigors of the road compromised the quality of that time.

The road held little interest for Anna Kate, who preferred to stay closer to her mom and home. Zak enjoyed being there a little more, but frankly, I believe John was distracted by their presence on tour. He tried melding the two worlds, but John's family away from home was the band and crew—and they demanded his full attention. Plus, when family members were introduced into that mix, I think the added responsibility of looking after them, or making sure they were taken care of, diluted some of the pleasure John found being on the road, doing his job and performing his music.

In the early days, through the mid-'70s, Annie would sometimes join John on tour, depending on the city we were playing. San Francisco seemed to lure her out of Aspen, as did New York, Washington, D.C., and Minneapolis, the latter two being her former hometowns. But life on the road, which was fast and chaotic, was never her thing, and she preferred to let John have his space there. When she did come along, she would usually bring Kris O'Connor's wife, Bonnie. They were very close in those early years. Annie and Bonnie were fun to be around, free of ego or pretense. When John had to say goodbye to Kris after our European tour around 1980, it really was a blow for both the Denvers and the O' Connors.

John met Kris in Washington, D.C., when Kris was managing the Cellar Door, a famous nightclub in Georgetown where John regularly entertained.

John composed and sang "Leaving on a Jet Plane" there, prior to it being released by Peter, Paul and Mary. "Take Me Home, Country Roads" was performed for Cellar Door patrons for the first time anywhere on December 30, 1970. Kris and John got to be buddies, and when John's career gained traction, he offered Kris the job as tour manager. Kris became John's right-hand man—they were inseparable—and together enjoyed the monetary fruits of their labor. Kris was a kind-hearted guy who had great organizational skills. He could get you from one end of the country to the other in a flash, even if you didn't have a dime in your pocket. He had the access and resources to fix even seemingly impossible situations. He was a natty dresser who ironed a crease in his Levi's and, no matter the temperature, wore a turtleneck. Woe to the person who called him before the crack of noon, too. He was a night owl and a late sleeper.

I really liked Kris, but on occasion we locked horns. During the '75 tour he called me out, saying I wasn't pulling my weight in tearing down the projection screens after a show. And it's true, I wasn't. But I was told that stagehands would handle that so I could make the bus along with everyone else for the plane to the next gig. After all, I wasn't part of the road crew. That was when John's band and tour crew grew from just a handful of guys to more than thirty. It was a road manager's nightmare. This incident caused some tension between us for a few weeks, and I think they even considered firing me. When I got wind of that, I decided to find a compromise. I talked to the stagehands, and we agreed that I'd do the hardest part of the job and get the teardown started, which took about fifteen minutes of my time. Then they'd finish it up—and I'd still make the bus. This worked for everyone, and things went back to normal.

Toward the end of that tour, John found me backstage and told me that the way I turned around that situation was one of the best parts of that tour for him. It surprised me that he made a point to tell me this, but I imagine having a problem solved without him having to get involved was a novelty that he appreciated.

Years later, in 1979 or 1980, at the end of a European tour, Kris was losing the battle against some personal demons. He looked horrible and could no longer handle the job he'd been so good at, which left John no choice but to replace him. Shortly after he was let go, he and his wife, Bonnie, pulled up their roots in Aspen and moved to the East Coast where Kris grew up. I didn't see Kris again for four or five years. Then one day I got a call from him. He was in Long Beach, and he invited me up to one of John's solo shows. Turns out, Kris was working for John again. He looked great; he had sobered up and was ready to jump back into his old job. But things had changed. He was no longer a partner in the business. His deal was very different, and so was working with John. But he soldiered on, still loyal and looking out for John's best interests. Kris served as road manager until John's death.

Four years after divorcing Annie, John, now thirty-eight, met Cassandra, a stunning Aussie blond, in a hotel bar. After a two-year courtship, they were married in 1988. Seemingly against all medical odds (since previous tests showed John had an extremely low sperm count and couldn't have children of his own), Cassandra gave birth to their daughter, Jesse Belle, in May 1989.

Cassandra became a fixture on the road, partly because she joined John onstage and sang vocals on one or two numbers, and partly because she was a free spirit. The road suited her in a way it never had for Annie, and I think John enjoyed having her at his side. But their marriage, fraught with claims of infidelity—this time made by John toward his wife—was short-lived. They separated in 1991 and divorced two years later. Although the road didn't seem to hold the same allure for John in those final years, the cheering and adoring audiences seemed to sustain him enough to keep a busy concert schedule.

And there were some positives, including John starting his own record label. A record label like RCA would contract with a musician to record a certain number of albums over a certain number of years. A typical contract at this time would have been a two-year deal with four albums. Aside from the production of the actual album, the label had artist reps (called A&R guys) who made the rounds to all the radio stations to promote their artists and give away records, and, if the artist was performing in town, perhaps give away concert tickets to the station as prizes for their listeners. Because the label's interest was solely in promoting the record album, they were pretty strict about keeping to a recording schedule for all the albums promised in the signed contract. It wasn't John making an album when he had the new songs and he felt like it; rather, it was John scrambling to meet the expectations of the label as per the contract agreement. (This is the reason, by the way, so many artists throw together Christmas albums—it's to fulfill their contracts.)

Because John now had his own label and was no longer tethered to a third-party recording contract, he could call his own shots and record when he felt he had a compelling product—that is, a solid list of new tunes. Of course, the downside of this is the lack of promotional support, which is why he had his own label but contracted the distribution of its products through RCA.

No longer reliant on a record label to promote him, he did his best to tour where he wanted and when he wanted, recording when he had enough tunes to record and when he felt ready, not when the label needed him to.

The venues by now were smaller than the 15,000-seat halls of previous years, and the crowds were not as big. But the smaller 2,500 to 5,000 seaters were more appropriate for John's newer shows anyway. More acoustic in nature, these theaters, which were more intimate for a single lead performer, were really the best place to see John do his work. And they were almost always sold out—twenty years after his last hit record. Remarkable.

Other changes were emerging in the mid-'90s as well. I think John was tired of mountain life, or maybe mountain life in and around Aspen. He was away more than ever. Although he was still committed to its causes, his passion for Windstar waned, or at least he didn't talk about it as much anymore. John didn't want Windstar to be a traditional nonprofit with a fundraising arm—he wanted to finance it himself so he could support the projects he wanted to support. It's a tough way to keep a nonprofit afloat, plus it takes a lot of personal energy when trying to take on an intractable, worldwide challenge like eradicating hunger. I suspect the enormous pressure of keeping it financed weighed on him, and a lot of the early personalities that seasoned its startup were now gone, including his friend and Windstar board of directors member Buckminster Fuller, who died in 1983. John was also putting more energy into individual efforts now, such as flying over the rainforests of Central America with his pilot and friend, Bruce Gordon, and documenting the loss of natural and ancient forestland.

About the time his marriage to Cassandra was unraveling, John put me up in the guest room in his house, a nice if sparsely furnished and uncluttered room. There was nothing in the drawers or closets, but oddly enough, right there on the dresser was a letter written from John to Cassandra.

It was strange. Why was this letter left in the guest room where I was staying? I read it because it seemed it had been left there for that purpose. The text was a rundown of all the things going on between the two of them, and the common issues that break up marriages. It was an "I can't deal with this anymore" letter.

I gave the letter to John later and said, "This was on my dresser." He said, "Oh yeah. Did you look at it?" A little sheepishly, I said, "Yeah." He said, "What did you think?" We talked about it, and I became even more convinced that it had been placed there for me to read. He had taken a circuitous and (for me) somewhat uncomfortable route, but he really just needed a friend.

It was on that visit to Aspen, and during the few hours we spent at the iconic Woody Creek Tavern (a dive bar where patrons played it cool when famous folks like Hunter S. Thompson and John came in), when he dropped a bombshell and first mentioned the idea of quitting the business. Retiring. He was burned out. It was all becoming uninspiring for him: the touring where fans were only interested in the old hits; the grind of producing new music that would sell; the constant scramble to try to stay in the public eye. He was feeling his age, and, while just in his early fifties then, John was also feeling less than relevant on the music scene. He didn't feel he had an audience anymore, or better said, he wasn't attracting a new audience. I felt he was undergoing a serious period of self-reflection when he doubted himself, his talent, and his commitment to his craft. Although it was a shock to hear him say the words out loud, it didn't completely surprise me. At that point, in our more than twenty years together, I had witnessed dozens of times when John felt doubt about himself and his music. Remember, he never felt welcomed by the other big stars of the era who felt his music was goody-two-shoes. He tried to pass this off as no big deal, but it hurt deeply. On top of that, he many times harbored his own personal doubts about songs and whether they were any good, especially in the beginning of his career when I came on board. These were the times he checked in with band members and others for validation. But this time, sitting on the bar stools at Woody Creek, seemed different. It felt like all the years of fighting those inner doubts and gremlins were starting to catch up with him. He just seemed plain tired.

When people start sharing life's dilemmas like this, I just try to listen and not interject a lot of ideas of my own. I gathered from that conversation that he didn't feel relevant to the culture anymore—a contrast to when college kids and audiences of the '70s caught the deeper meaning of his songs—and that hurt him the most. Audiences these days were just too cynical and superficial—and producers seemed to be looking for pop hits made with digital synthesizers and electronic drums. He thought he had been writing some of his best material and it wasn't being heard. Musical tastes were changing, and he was unwilling and unable to keep up with them. It was frustrating, and he wasn't sure what to do going forward. He continued to perform in concerts, but his now older audience was there to hear the hits—although he always threw in some new stuff to keep it interesting for himself. In the old days touring was fun because we were all younger and carefree—it was like camp. Now it was more of a grind.

Years before he was a professional musician, John created a vision of what he would do if he became famous. It was almost as if he wished this life on himself. All his energy through the years was put toward creating a flurry of activity around that vision to make it come to be. John's philosophy was that we are all responsible for everything that happens to us. He didn't have any problem reveling in the kudos for what had gone right—and he felt the personal pain when something went wrong.

He'd been drinking a lot around that time, and it was common for him to consume an entire bottle of Stoli vodka after a concert. I remember going into a Windstar meeting once after a concert at the historic Fox Theatre in St. Louis in 1992. I'd flown in specifically for this meeting. We were going over some licensing issues, and our merchandise man, Dave Furano, was also there. John and Dave generally got along well enough, but John was always apprehensive about exploitation when his name was attached to merchandise. Dave's job was to market and sell John Denver as a product, which John understood, but John was cautious about everything, including his personal business ventures.

The meeting grew progressively antagonistic between the two, while I just sat at the table listening in discomfort. John had some wine right after the show with dinner, which he took into his dressing room. And then he started in on the Stoli, and that is when the nicest, most professional guy in the world—John—suddenly got mean and exploded in anger at Dave.

Given the distance and perspective time provides, I now see it as an overreaction for being pushed too far by Dave to monetize the John Denver name and image. Dave, Hal Thau, John, and I were the principals for Windstar Licensing. My job was to create interest in products we could sell at concerts, such as T-shirts and recordings of *Earth Songs* that couldn't be found anywhere else. Those items made sense. Dave, though, had no qualms in pitching anything from BBQ sauce to G.I. Joe–type dolls bearing John's likeness. It was in that meeting when John drew the line—and let his anger show. Again, I think it was a reaction to feeling he was becoming irrelevant and just another piece of commerce—reduced to a plastic toy.

That's not to say that there weren't times when John felt it made sense to lend his music and voice to commercial endeavors. Coors used the song "Rocky Mountain High" in commercials to go with the tagline of the beer being "born in the Rockies." John drank Coors, so giving permission to use his song made sense. He also made a commercial with Post Raisin Bran. I was with him in LA where the spot was made, and it was right up his alley—being shown in a cabin with his dog eating a natural, healthy cereal. What made John wary was attaching his name to or using his music with a product that he might later come to regret because he didn't believe in what the company stood for. That weighed on his commercial decision-making more than any amount of money ever could. He had no interest in running up his net worth with unvetted commercial endorsements. He lived, albeit most comfortably, within his personal budget and never went overboard with all the things money could buy. It was important to him that he could afford to say no to even the most lucrative of deals if they weren't right and on-brand.

Back to the meeting with Dave in St. Louis when John exploded. I'd been close to John personally and professionally for more than twenty years by that point, and this was way out of character. "John being mean" was something new. I felt he was headed down a dangerous path.

It's an interesting scenario: a problem that developed and worsened later in life and not during his most stress-filled, high-profile years. Phil Collins wrote in his autobiography that he used drugs and alcohol with no real problem during all those years he was on the road with Genesis; he waited until his fifties to become a full-blown alcoholic. John's situation was similar: No one could deny any longer that John had a problem with alcohol.

John never had a substance-abuse problem of any sort in the '70s and early '80s, as far as I could tell, despite bouts of depression, particularly around the time of the death of his father in 1982, his divorce from Annie shortly thereafter, and the end of his long-time management relationship with Jerry Weintraub. And then came the loss of his RCA recording contract after more than sixteen years with the label. That was a pretty bad year!

First up was the split from Jerry. In my opinion, John had been coddled by Jerry for years. John was Jerry's special project—a talent Jerry believed he cooked from scratch. Now that he was a star and had fulfilled all of Jerry's ambitions for him, Jerry had moved on to new challenges in new entertainment arenas. John didn't feel like he was getting enough of Jerry's time and attention—and wasn't sure he needed it anymore anyway. Jerry had grown his client list to include Neil Diamond, Frank Sinatra, and others, not to mention his foray into producing movies. At first, John was okay with Jerry's new challenges, but when Jerry stopped dropping everything to take John's calls, that hurt.

John felt he had made Jerry. Jerry felt he had made John. But regardless of who made whom, John wasn't producing and selling hit records like he used to. He was no longer in demand for guest appearances on television, and it had been years since his hit film debut in *Oh, God!* with nothing to back it up. He could see his career arc bending downward, and he didn't like it.

To compound his frustration, John was having problems with RCA, his longtime record label. He had just completed recording a new album at RCA in Los Angeles. Typically, Jerry would give it a listen and give it his stamp of approval before release. There might be a song or two he'd want John to take another swing at or maybe swap out for others.

But this time Jerry hated the whole thing.

Jerry felt it was an old sound, a tired formula, and no longer relevant to audiences. His fix was to go full-out country with John, rather than continue trying to straddle the worlds of country and pop. So, John reluctantly moved to Tennessee for a couple of months to record a Nashville-sounding album and found what he already knew: The South wasn't at all his world. It moved too slow for him with too much rehearsal—he preferred the faster pace of New York and Los Angeles. He also felt as if he was being forced to join the country crowd, a place he never felt he belonged.

John was at a crossroads with his career, his marriage, and his management. It was a lot to ponder. His career needed a new direction, that was clear, but he was reluctant to do what others were pressuring him to do. He felt Jerry, like his father, had too much say in his life. So, like his escape from home when he was eighteen years old, he escaped Jerry's grip on his life by firing him. It was not a happy separation. And, unlike his departure from home when he was a teen, no one chased after him to bring him back. John found himself alone, adrift, and uncertain of what to do.

RCA dropped him for the usual reason: Sales were bad. There was also a change in RCA's management. From John's perspective, the record label wasn't as committed as he would have liked. He wanted to do his next album *his* way, so he launched Windsong Records, first as a subsidiary of RCA. When John split from the label, it became an independent label named Windstar Records. It was this label that produced the *Earth Songs* album, which was sold only at concerts and is my personal favorite.

But this was a dark time for all of us, when the road definitely got rocky. John was not a fun guy to be around and wasn't his gregarious old self. He was either in a foul mood, or worse, he'd go silent. As sometimes happens, it was the people he was closest to who he was the rudest to—he didn't feel he had to hide his problems. He'd snap at those still around him for seemingly no reason. Or, even worse, he'd go into bouts of silence where he didn't say a word and instead was lost in his own thoughts and anger. He seemed upset with himself and the world. A lot was happening, and when your personal philosophy dictates that you're responsible for everything that happens to you, that's a heavy load to bear. Most of us lost some degree of access to him, and, to find anything out, we resorted to buddying up to one of his assistants, who was often just in the dark like everyone else. If you know his music, it doesn't take a lot of detective work to figure out when this dark period of time was. His songwriting took a hard rudder right with songs like "Falling Out of Love" in 1983.

For John, the heartbreak of the end of his marriage to Cassandra was a catalyst for a serious downward spiral. On the day their divorce was finalized in 1993, John and Cassandra had a friendly dinner together at a restaurant in Aspen. On his way home, John was arrested for driving under the influence of alcohol. A year to the day later, John smashed his 1963 Porsche 356 into a tree after a Scotch-fueled bar night in Aspen. With the second DUI, the judge gave John a suspended sentence with community service. But he also lost his driver's license and, more importantly to John, his pilot's license.

It was about a year later when John was trying to move on from Cassandra and stabilize his life that I was finding some different work in showbiz. Or, should I say, I was on the edge of an opportunity. Tim Swift, a friend who was a producer, had a booking that seemed perfect for John. Tim wanted me to ask him to participate, and there was a percentage in the deal for me if John said yes. The gig? The grand opening of the Bluegrass Music Hall of Fame & Museum in Kentucky.

Best of all, it would be an easy appearance for John: Just show up with the band and do a forty-minute set. Also on the bill was a rising new star by the name of Alison Krauss, along with other bluegrass and country legends. I think the deal was a $50,000 guarantee, all expenses paid. I had to use a fair amount of persuasion to talk John into it, but eventually he agreed. He made me work for it, but I think he said yes because he knew it would be good for me in a new role I was taking on as a concert promoter. It cut into a vacation trip John had planned to Alaska, but he took on the gig anyway and had a great time—although I never heard the end of it about him missing the start of his trip. It meant a lot to me and showed the kindness and real loyalty John was capable of to those he worked with.

There seemed to be only specific times when John felt happy. That event in Kentucky was one. Directly after that he left for that fishing trip in Alaska where he could enjoy his love of Mother Nature. And, of course, any time he spent with his kids was a highlight for him. He was still reeling from his divorce from Cassandra, who had moved to Los Angeles, taking their young daughter Jesse Belle with her; and, I believe, he never fully recovered from his split with Annie more than a decade earlier.

Just before his death in 1997, John conducted a frank interview with the *Telegraph* and said, "Divorce is just the most awful thing in the world." And for him, it really was. He had loved both his wives, and he deeply loved his three children. To his way of thinking, he had taken his marriages as seriously as everything else he'd ever done. Those failures broke his heart.

From my perspective, whenever you divorce someone, especially someone you had been with for so long (you could say Annie was the love of John's life), you first look for redemption. You ask questions like, "How can I make this better?" or "How can I make this right?" Most times redemption doesn't come, so just the cold fact of failure remains. It's a pain you learn to live with and one that—hopefully—will ease with the passing of time. Sometimes a change of scenery helps, which is one of the reasons John left Aspen and moved to Monterey, California. He was seeking a fresh start.

The home in Aspen that had been so lovingly built over those years and enjoyed by his growing family was left empty. Uncertain of what to do with it, he kept it, although he was living 1,200 miles away and 7,000 feet lower in altitude on the Pacific Coast. He rarely traveled to Aspen anymore. Only after his death did the family decide to sell the Starwood estate that had held all of my fond memories of John Denver, the family man.

Without its famous owner and his personal possessions, the house seemed a hard sell, so it sat on the market for months. It was such a personal home, full of joyous memories. So much of it was designed the way John lived his life: free, open, with abundant light and a picture-postcard view of the Rocky Mountains from every window.

But it had its share of skeletons hiding among the vaulted ceilings. This space, as beautiful a sanctuary as it was, was the scene of the violent and ugly side of John, the part of him hidden from view that I had the misfortune to witness on occasion. In one episode, a fit of destructive anger overtook John and he took a chainsaw to Annie's kitchen counter—with Annie present and terrified that she would be next. It was an unfathomable act of retaliation aimed at her because she had removed some trees from the property while he was away.

He tells it in detail in his autobiography. When I first heard of it from Kris O'Connor, years before John published the story in his book, I wasn't shocked. Something dark had been brewing in John for months; anyone who knew him recognized it. I figured at some point he would explode—I just didn't know how it would manifest itself. It wasn't surprising to me that someone close to him pissed him off and precipitated such an eruption. What was disturbing is that he lost his temper so violently in Annie's presence, but, in his book, he seemed to pass it off as a simple expression of anger when, really, it signaled something much worse.

I felt that John's anger was being fueled by too much alcohol consumption, in addition to all the losses. His life wasn't great, and although he was still functioning, he was spinning out of control. He hadn't hit bottom—but he was close enough to smell it.

I was still in John's orbit, but we were not as close as we once were. I had not been to his California home and saw him just a few times a year. We'd usually meet in LA or in whatever city he was in for work, and I'd show him proofs of a program booklet or an album design so he could give his approval.

Now starting fresh in Monterey, John acknowledged that drinking was part of the problem and he did a month-long stint in rehab. John lived in a house on the famous 17-Mile Drive. This placed him physically closer to Jesse Belle, now just entering school age. It was easy for him to take his tiny experimental Rutan Long-EZ plane (he owned three other larger planes, including a Learjet) down to see her in Los Angeles or to fly her back to his home—a quick hop. The celebrated Pebble Beach Golf Links was near his new place, and John played with Clint Eastwood and other new friends in his new environment. On his fateful flight in the Rutan on October 12, 1997, he was intending to buzz over Eastwood's house for fun.

It's worth noting here that he was still flying without a valid pilot's license. But according to the autopsy provided by the FAA, there were no drugs or alcohol in John's system when he took that fatal flight. It seemed that when John Denver took to the skies, all he had been doing to numb himself from the pain of divorce, loneliness, and more was left behind.

Relaxing at home. Photo courtesy Lowell Norman.

Chapter 11

THE ENDLESS SEARCH

I wrote this book over a period of a couple of years. At one point, I felt that—for the most part—it was finished. But something nagged at me, saying it wasn't quite done. Something was missing, something was left out. Then it dawned on me that what was missing was the one thing that drove John and inspired much of his songwriting. The thing that motivated him to public service. The thing that kept him on his search for truth.

Because John was a searcher. He would often refer to himself as such. Not so much a lost soul but a seeking, wandering, and searching one. I mentioned in an earlier chapter about how, during an afternoon tour through his boyhood town of Tucson, John pointed out his old Presbyterian church and said, "That's where I met God." Even though there was some wryness in his voice, there was also some truth.

It was where he met God, and it also was where he started his search.

John was pretty locked in on where he stood philosophically. His politics were socially liberal for his time. He didn't budge much on his principles. He was strong, for instance, on his responsibility to protect the planet. He was committed wholeheartedly to the notion that living in a world where hunger exists is immoral. There was no wiggle room for him on these issues. But when it came to matters of the soul, the source of truth, the definition or concept of God, he was as wide open and welcoming as any searcher could be.

The source of much of John's philosophy came from the ancient Chinese manuscript the *I Ching* (which translates to "Book of Changes"), originally composed 3,000 years ago by Taoist masters, whose understanding of life closely matches how modern physics describes it today. The authors were inspired by natural processes and articulated how nature can be a teacher. The *I Ching* traveled with John everywhere he went. He often read it on the plane as we toured. He quoted it often. Much of his philosophy on life was directly inspired by its teachings.

The *I Ching* is not a religious text; it is simply an ancient understanding of the forces at work in the world around us. Deep study in the liturgy of those forces, however, can become a sort of religion. For instance, the idea that the earth is our mother—a prevalent concept in John's songwriting— comes from his understanding of the *I Ching*.

This book is about my own memories of life traveling and working with John, so I can't presume to fully represent John's deepest convictions. My experiences with John regarding philosophy and religion are just moments in time, conversations, and observances I made over the years I was near him. Huge pieces of this part of the puzzle are missing.

I first witnessed John's search in the early days of our touring together. I kept hearing about something called est (Erhard Seminars Training). I fig- ured it was a self-exploration training of some sort but couldn't fully under- stand what all the fuss was about. The only folks I knew who had taken est training were John, Annie, and Steve Weisberg, and they had all adopted a new lexicon with phrases that made no sense unless you had taken the train- ing. All I really understood about the training was that there wasn't anything to understand about the training! That's the kind of sense it made to me.

After a year or so of asking questions, seeking a better understanding, John called me one day and told me he had gifted me a scholarship to take the training, which I completed in the winter of 1975. I can't say it spoke to me like it had to the others, but at least now the language made better sense.

The training was capable of doing some positive things for you, if you were receptive to change. The most important thing it did, through its rather unorthodox process, was force you to confront your fears and deal with all the obstacles you've created to keep yourself from dealing with those fears. I know for John—because he articulated this to me and others—this was a huge issue in his life. It also provided you with the understanding that you, and you alone, are responsible for everything that happens in your life. It's something that I still can't fully grasp, but I do understand what a freeing concept this could be.

The other thing that est provided John was an introduction to its founder, Werner Erhard. Werner was a charismatic, larger–than-life character. He had a mystical aura about him that he worked to his strong advantage.

Before every meeting, Werner was briefed on who was attending. He memorized the names, and visualized the person based on information he would get ahead of the meeting, such as your size and personal characteristics—details of your face, beard, glasses, etc. He would walk up to you (as he did to me when we first met), look in your eyes and say your name, and then introduce himself. Very disconcerting when you don't expect that kind of personal recognition. Also, very engaging. I was around Werner several times and watched him work a room. He was a master at this. He also had a way of shining. He looked polished and scrubbed to the point of almost being saintly. He was effective, articulate, and intimidating in his presentation. He was, in every sense of the word, the consummate salesman. These qualities in him, along with his reimagining of Eastern philosophy, helped kick off the me decade of the '70s. Werner was New Age before it had a name.

I believe John's experience of est and subsequent friendship with Werner ignited his interest in spiritual matters and inspired many of the songs he penned during the '70s. It helped John frame feelings he always had but didn't know how to articulate. John's *Spirit* album is, in many ways, the culmination of ideas and philosophies he found while navigating through his search during those years.

With Werner also came the formation of The Hunger Project and the idea that ending hunger in the world was an idea whose time had come. It was a concept that John fully endorsed, and one that drove his public commitment to ending hunger.

Along with this public commitment came a private one: Meditation became a part of John's day. When at home, he would often meditate under a large, open-framed brass pyramid. It occupied a room of the office that was attached to the guesthouse. He would sit in the lotus position in the exact center of the pyramid for an hour or so at a time.

John was, in every sense of the term, a New Ager. He might not have liked the term—disliked being categorized or pigeonholed as part of a particular group—but he certainly embraced much of that culture.

At the same time, he very much respected traditional values and more orthodox forms of spiritual expression. He often commented on how he wished he could simply accept the Christian faith of his youth as his truth. He admired and was totally accepting of others who practiced traditional conventional religion. But, as he would say, "It just doesn't work for me." He had many friends who were clergy of one faith or another, and many of his best personal friends were quite devout. When I had dinner with astronaut Charlie Duke's family at John's house, John, in a nod to Charlie's Christian faith, asked for a blessing. When he met the pope, he asked for the pontiff's blessing. So much for being pigeonholed. As John would say, speaking of the myriad religious beliefs, "It all comes from the same space."

But John was always about the search for something new, something he hadn't yet experienced. When John made the *Different Directions* album (released in 1991), the recording was all done at a studio in Omaha, Nebraska, belonging to Chip Davis (of Mannheim Steamroller fame). American Gramophone had become John's new label.

I was out in Omaha toward the end of those recording sessions to shoot the cover for the album. John had one of the studios set up with his chair in the middle of the room surrounded by various crystals of varying sizes and shapes. I'd heard that John had recently been investigating the potential power of crystals and how their vibration could enhance creative abilities, but this was the first time I had seen it in practice.

It was also on that trip that I first became aware of John's interest in the ancient practice of cleromancy (the casting of lots). In this practice, objects such as sticks and coins are thrown, and where and how they land provide clues about the future.

His search took him to China to better understand the Buddhist culture; it took him to tribal ceremonies of the American Indians; it took him to readings; it took him to seances; and it took him to mediums who claimed to channel ancient wise men.

It would be pure speculation on my part to elaborate too much on any of this. I only know that these were all part of his search. I also know that most of this came at a particularly vulnerable time in his life, after his divorce with Annie, after his father died, and as his time at the top of the charts was ending.

I think, in the end, his search took him back to the mountains, nature, and his home. That was where he had always drawn his energy from, where he had found his center, where he had discovered his inspiration. All the rest was a sideshow, a distraction. And although he had moved to be next to the ocean, he could not bring himself to sell his home high above Aspen.

So perhaps I have shed a little light on just one of the origins of John's philosophy of life. There are many more. I believe that John subscribed to a rather large and tall menu of philosophies and disciplines, a virtual smorgasbord of ideas and concepts that never seemed to run out, but that still left him unfulfilled, searching for more. There seemed to be a never-ending trail of new and increasingly esoteric concepts for John.

The journey, the search, was long, and it had many turns. But in the end, I'm not so sure it was all that far from his boyhood church in Tucson, Arizona, where he seemed to both know a truth and question it.

John doing a little fingerpickin' on the mandolin. Photo courtesy Lowell Norman.

Chapter 12

FINAL FLIGHT

The warm fall day near Monterey, California, was reportedly clear and the skies calm. It was Sunday, the kind of day when you might want to get up early and play a round of golf at Spyglass Hill with friends. That was what John had done with his morning on that October day.

He had also planned to spend the afternoon "flying my new bird." He had just picked up the plane and had taken some lessons on Saturday in Santa Maria before flying it up to Monterey and its new hangar.

On Sunday, after practicing touch-and-go at the Monterey Peninsula Airport, he got clearance to take his new plane for a one-hour spin. After he was up in the air, the controllers in the tower were having difficulty tracking him and asked John to change his radar frequency. After fiddling with his radio for a moment, he contacted the tower at 5:28 p.m., asking, "Do you have it now?" Those would be his last known words.

The rest of John's day has become clouded in speculation and misinformation. Here is what I know, which has come from credible sources and trusted friends who spoke with him in the days prior to the crash.

First, John was in a great state of mind. His demons and the struggles he had fought so hard to control in his life during the early '90s were now behind him. Annie reported that he seemed happier than at any other recent time. The move to Monterey from Aspen seemed indeed to signify the beginning of a new chapter in his life. For those couple of years, the only hiking he wanted to do now was on the sunny fairways of California.

His son, Zak, now in his early twenties, was building a life for himself just down the valley from Aspen in Basalt. His older daughter, Anna Kate, just two years younger than Zak, was also beginning to make her way and was starting her degree at Dartmouth College. Annie and John were on friendlier terms, and all the rancor around his divorce from Cassandra had settled down. Being only a short flight away from Jesse Belle in LA was added value.

John had renewed interest from recording labels and had just completed a children's album. He had friends from the Bay Area in addition to his golfing buddies at home. New business and professional opportunities that he had been working on were beginning to ripen. He was playing with a new band, musicians mostly from Nashville, and he was planning more tours.

After shopping for a more economical airplane (both for his commute to LA and to get Jesse Belle on weekends), he settled on the unusual-looking Rutan-designed plane known as a Long-EZ. It was a tandem two-seater light airplane, built from a homemade kit by the original owner, with a fuel-saving Lycoming 150-horsepower engine. The engine and propeller are in the back of the plane and push it along. It has long wings, but instead of a traditional tail, it has canards, or small forewings, near the pilot canopy. It had an excellent safety record. Since its introduction in the early 1980s, more than 2,000 planes have been built from kits by aviation hobbyists. This particular plane was now on its second owner, who lived just down the coast in Santa Maria. This was where John first saw it and took it for a spin. He bought it, had it repainted, and flew it to its new home in Monterey.

Soon after he took off alone on that fateful Sunday, we know he had some fuel in tank one and a full tank in tank two. We also know he had commandeered a pair of vice grips from a mechanic to assist in turning the fuel switch, should he need to switch tanks while he was aloft. The switch had been placed in an awkward position behind his left shoulder and was scheduled to be moved to a better location soon.

Long-EZs were considered experimental planes, mainly because they were not mass-produced but rather built one at a time by private builders who could customize some of the controls to fit their personal tastes or needs. This switch placement made no sense to anyone except to the builder and first owner.

As John was practicing takeoffs and landings in his new plane, my family and I had coincidentally been visiting the Monterey Bay Aquarium and were heading home to Irvine, California. I had no idea what John was doing and, since we didn't have a project in progress, I hadn't spoken to him in a couple of weeks. We arrived home just after dark and hadn't been in the house for five minutes when the phone rang. It was our friend and neighbor Ann Strain asking if I had heard the news. She was uncertain if it was true, but there were reports that John and his plane had crashed in the surf in Monterey. No one knew his fate.

I immediately called John's cell number and got his voicemail. I left a message saying that there were reports of an accident, and I hoped this was not accurate and that all was well. I tried again half an hour later. Soon after, we all heard the detailed reports on television, followed moments later by a call from Kris O'Connor detailing what exactly had been reported to him. The crash was confirmed by the FAA, and within hours we got the final news: John was gone.

The official FAA report, published after an exhaustive and time-consuming investigation, concluded that pilot error caused the accident. The theory is that the engine sputtered as the plane was starving for fuel. John, turning to switch tanks, inadvertently added pressure to the rudder pedals with his leg and maybe moved the joystick, too, which put the plane in a sudden and unforgiving attitude, so it was no longer aerodynamic and slipped through the air. Trained pilots will tell you (and indeed I had heard this from John on more than one occasion) that planes go down because two or three things happen at once—a perfect storm of error that compounds whatever the original problem was. That seemed to play out here.

The theory makes sense, but that doesn't stop the whys from being asked by fans, friends, and loved ones, even now. Why was the fuel tank switch in such an odd place? Why wasn't he keeping an eye on the gauges? He knew all the things that could go wrong, so why wasn't he paying more attention? We'll never know.

On one hand, the news shocked me—it seemed so hard to believe. But in another way, it was something I had always feared deep down, and in a way, expected. How long can we tempt fate before she catches up to us? John did it all the time in his adventures. He pushed the envelope—safely usually, but not always.

It didn't take long before various news organizations called me asking for photos. Every media outlet nationally and internationally was covering the tragedy and needed visual content. The following week was busy as I provided *People* and other news organizations with photos of John; it was a sad and emotionally exhausting task.

A few days later my wife, Deb, and I flew to Denver for the funeral, and then up to Aspen to be with friends at the memorial service. The memorial service was a fitting end to the week as the shock and sadness over John's death had been replaced by an opportunity to celebrate his life. Each member of John's family spoke, and a flutist played a hauntingly beautiful melody that flowed over the thousands who were there on the crisp mid-October day. The singer-songwriter Lyle Lovett, the only celebrity to attend, sang and spoke about how John impacted him and his work. Indeed, in a May 2022 *Forbes* magazine article, Lovett listed all of the musical influences in his life, saying, "Those kinds of singer-songwriters who would be classified as Americana these days, that was pop music. That was important to me. To hear John Denver play, to see John Denver on his television specials in my high school years, stand on national TV and play a song with just his guitar, and for it to sound complete and beautiful and emotional, that was important to me."

I was overwhelmed with emotion because the memorial tribute was so well done. I hadn't seen some of those people in years, and it was moving to reconnect and hear stories about John, some that I hadn't heard before. Annie recounted one I did know—and that was about how John would have really liked seeing all these people here celebrating his life. He was a guy who spent his whole life not understanding how much people liked and admired him. That belief stemmed from a childhood where he didn't have a lot of friends, so it was hard for him to acknowledge that people could feel so deeply about him. It was more than fans adoring him—it was an outpouring of love and recognition of his great talent and what he stood for in life.

Annie hosted a reception later for all his friends and family at the Hotel Jerome, the oldest hotel in Aspen. After that, a couple dozen of us ended up around a fire in the backyard at her house and told stories about John late into the night. For most of us who worked with him, that was the last time we were all together.

I've had years to think it all over, to try to make sense of his death and the timing of it. He had in many ways reclaimed his life. He had made some positive and healing decisions, including moving to California. His career was still intact and a new album (for which he posthumously won his only Grammy, with his nine-year-old daughter, Jesse Belle, accepting the award) had just been completed.

If his career was not what it had once been, his voice was as crystalline as ever, and through the trials and pain of the previous years, you had to believe those final songs were incubating—just waiting to be written. His other voice, the one that spoke of a healthy environment, the end of world hunger, and of a sustainable and prosperous future, was still respected and strong. He had stirred action in the hearts and minds of so many people, and his passions would live on in the good work they would do for years to come.

John had always been a zealous activist, a symbol for all things natural and humane; it was a badge he wore proudly his entire public life. The songs had been the vessels, the means to getting his message across, a message that he delivered a full two decades before terms like *climate change, environmentalist*, and *recycling* became part of our everyday vernacular.

In a way it could be argued that there was an elegance to how John spent the final minutes of his life. Soaring with the eagle and the hawk, he had to be smiling from his place in the sky about where he was and the unlikely journey he had taken to get there.

John posing on his vintage 1931 biplane. On April 21, 1989, he had an accident in this plane as he was taxiing down the runway at Holbrook Municipal Airport in Holbrook, Arizona. Photo courtesy John Denver photo archive.

EPILOGUE

Passion for Flight

When I first started working with John, he had neither a pilot's license nor an airplane. In fact, his initial interest in learning to fly came during those days in the mid-'70s when we were leasing business jets to get from town to town for our concert dates.

On one of those flights, I mentioned to the pilots my interest in learning to fly. After a few more conversations of that ilk, they presented me with a brand new Jeppesen instruction manual. The Jeppesen manual contained everything you need to know to pass ground school. I had it for about two days when John asked if he could borrow it. I never saw it again.

Within two years John not only had his pilot's license but also his instrument rating. He could fly multi-engine jet aircraft. Oh, and he had purchased a brand-new Learjet 35 and learned to fly it himself with the help of his own personal flight instructor, retired US Air Force Lieutenant Colonel Henry John Deutschendorf Sr.—his father.

John wanted to go beyond flying planes though—he had his eyes set on the stars. His dream was to be an astronaut. He had a longtime interest in space and in NASA, in particular. He applied for NASA's civilians-in-space program and had at least one moonwalker believing he had the chops.

Charlie Duke, the lunar module pilot of *Apollo 16*, and the tenth of the twelve people who have walked on the surface of the moon, hosted him for a behind-the-scenes look at the launch of the *Apollo-Soyuz* in the summer of 1975. And John Denver had questions. "We talked a lot about moon flights and astronauts," said Charlie Duke. "I worked on five of the nine missions to the moon, so I had a lot of knowledge of the crews and operations and mission control. He just absorbed it like a sponge.

"I think John would've given his right arm to go into space. He was a musician, but in his heart, he wanted to be an astronaut," said Duke.

* * *

At 8:38 a.m. on the morning of January 28, 1986, I was lying on an emergency room hospital bed, thankful that the morphine just put into my vein was kicking in. I had a kidney stone. I knew the symptoms well by now, having had more than a dozen since age twelve. Rarely were they so painful that I needed to get to the ER for treatment, but this time I had no choice. The pain was too great.

Six hours in, as I floated in and out of my morphine bliss, my attention was drawn to the television hanging in the corner of the room. The sound was up just enough to hear the countdown: ". . . four, three, ignition sequence starts, two, one . . . we have liftoff of the twenty-fifth space shuttle *Challenger*."

Like John, I was a NASA nerd, so I was suddenly glued to the television. Though I was falling into a euphoric state from the pain medication, I stayed focused on the monitor as the shuttle rose far into the sky. It was beautiful, inspiring, and dramatic. And then it exploded.

It was like a dream that suddenly became a nightmare. Did the shuttle just blow up? It had. And with it all seven crew members, including the first civilian in space, schoolteacher Christa McAuliffe. As someone who followed the space program, I knew all about her already. But also, I knew of her because John was at one time a candidate to be on this very shuttle mission—maybe in that very seat.

As a key proponent and initiator of the civilians-in-space initiative, John did make the very short list of potential shuttle passengers before President

Reagan announced the seat would be occupied by a teacher. John had passed all the NASA requirements and the rigorous astronaut physical exams. And he was, of course, a multi-engine jet pilot and amateur astronomer. Also, he was John Denver, beloved entertainer, loved by millions across generations.

Although disappointed in the president's decision to choose a teacher specifically, John continued to support the chosen crew and the civilians-in-space program. He got to know Christa and the other members of the crew. So, like me in that hospital bed and like all Americans who watched this tragedy unfold, John was devastated.

But for him, it was personal.

A few months later, I got a call from John, who was recording in Los Angeles. He wanted me to come up from my home in Orange County—to discuss an idea he had for a music video.

When I got to the studio, he played a new song he had written that was inspired by his feelings about the loss of the *Challenger* crew, titled "Flying for Me." It was beautiful. Up until then, I hadn't known the extent of his involvement with the shuttle program in general and the crew in particular, but I soon learned just how deeply he had been affected by the tragedy. He wanted to do something for the families, and writing and singing songs was what he did best, so "Flying for Me" was for them.

John asked me if I'd go to NASA and procure whatever footage I could to make a music video for the new song. I agreed. I knew right away that this would be a labor of love for me.

I had a week to get my assignment done, so I made my way to the film and video archive library at the Johnson Space Center in Houston to begin my research. The NASA librarian, who had been a fixture there since its inception, helped me navigate my way through the millions of feet of archived film and video. Everyone there was eager to help—they knew John was a proponent of NASA and all it stood for.

One of NASA's greatest products was the film and video images obtained during the various space missions. All of it is public domain, meaning anyone could use it without cost or special permission. It was a rich resource for me, and it seems I was the only one interested in mining it that week.

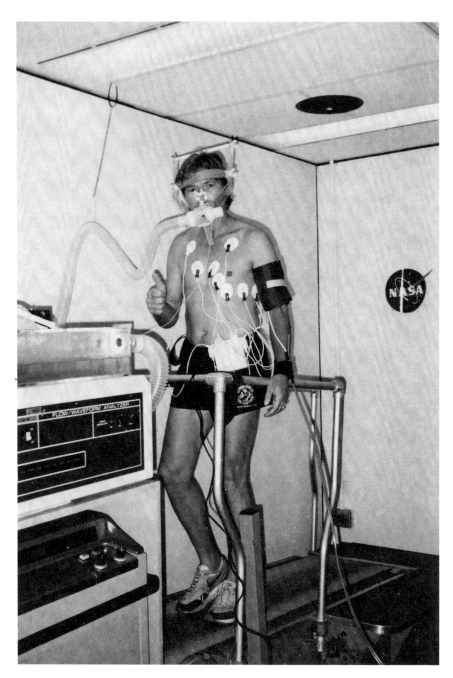

John was instrumental in the formation of NASA's civilians-in-space program. Part of his interest was, of course, to become the first civilian in space and the ride was all but assured until President Reagan chose a teacher, Christa McAuliffe, for that seat. Photo courtesy John Denver photo archive.

While there, I got to satisfy my inner NASA nerd in a number of ways, such as going to the Outpost—a famous bar where the astronauts hung out back during NASA's heyday. The walls were filled with classic photos and memorabilia from NASA's history. (Sadly, the Outpost closed its doors in 2010 and was destroyed by a fire a few months later, although the owner was able to get most of the memorabilia out before it went up in flames.)

I also got a feel for what it would be like to be an astronaut, something I had been wondering about since I read science magazines front to back as a kid. I spent part of one afternoon in the shuttle simulator, and in an entire shuttle spacecraft where I could sit at the controls. Sitting in one of the astronaut seats of the flight deck, I was oddly comforted that the explosion on *Challenger* would have been instantaneous, and the crew never knew what hit them. Up to that point, it was the most devastating accident in NASA's history. Although twenty-four shuttle missions had been completed with no problems, all missions were put on hold for two years while an investigation and redesigns were implemented.

The shuttle was really '60s technology. As I sat there on the flight deck in 1986, the shuttle was more than ten years old already. The computer on board was not nearly as powerful as my first-generation Macintosh computer. Today's iPhones are thousands of times more powerful.

So, imagine the faith the astronauts must have had in the relatively primitive technology to risk their lives in the name of exploration. It really brought home the fact that, although we've been space traveling now for more than fifty years, we really are just pioneers in covered wagons heading down an uncharted dusty trail.

After I had tagged all the images and film footage I needed copies of, I said goodbye and went home to piece together the music video. While I was in Los Angeles editing the film footage, I got a call from John wanting an update. After listening to the song a thousand times, I had a real feel for how I wanted to interpret the lyrics into images.

My idea was that the song was more than a tribute to the lost crew. It was a show of respect to all those who had volunteered to endure the challenges of space to benefit and speed the progress of science and technology for all humankind. So much of today's technology is a direct result of inventions we created to go into space, and the astronauts were the ones who made it all possible. I told John that I saw the song as a tribute to the whole of space exploration in general with a special spotlight on the *Challenger* crew. He agreed, but he also wanted me to put the explosion footage in the video. I was adamant—I didn't want to show that part, and instead, I just wanted to show the craft taking off and flying up and out of frame. Then I would place the faces of the crew individually against a sky of space, as if their spirits were still flying for us, as the song suggested.

And that is what I did. I went from Alan Shepard and his first flight all the way to the *Challenger* liftoff. Then I included spectacular images shot by the astronauts themselves, from Mercury to Gemini, Apollo to *Challenger*. It was one of my best creative efforts—and one where I didn't shoot a single frame of the original film.

John used that video in concert from 1986 until his own all too similar death in the skies over Monterey, California, in November 1997.

After John's memorial service in Aspen, I met a woman who introduced herself as one of the widows of the *Challenger* crew. She went on and on about how much John had meant to the crew, how involved he was in the healing of the families through the benefits and concerts he had performed. She also talked about how beautiful the song was and how sensitively he had created its music video. She said those images will never leave her memory. I didn't tell her that I had made the video for John. There was no need. She didn't know it, but in that moment, she had made all the effort worth it.

Years later, my family and I took a trip to Los Angeles to see John in concert. The backstage reunion was a mix of what you get when you meet an old friend again after years of being apart—an almost palpable feeling of the familiar and unknown. John was running on adrenaline from just getting offstage. We huddled together for a group hug and presented him with a sought-after doll for his youngest daughter, Jesse Belle. Before moving onto the next group, John excitedly told us of an opportunity he was pursuing to fly into space with the Russians, one he was confident would happen. Some could view his declaration and assuredness with cynicism, but it reminded me of our first meeting and his childlike eagerness about life and the opportunities for adventure it presented.

Tragedies happen. Nowhere is this more apparent than within the art and science of flight; the spark that caused the devastating fire in the oxygen-soaked capsule of *Apollo 1*; unusually cold temperatures that led to the failure of O-rings meant to protect those aboard the space shuttle *Challenger*; or a convergence of almost freakish errors that caused a proven pilot to plummet to his death. Human beings may temporarily join the stars and the hawks and eagles in flight, yet we're reminded there is a price to pay for pursuing such dreams. Our heroes both inspire us with their triumphs and fail us with their mistakes. And we are left to tell the story.

John Denver's Learjet 35 parked at the Aspen airport. Photo courtesy Lowell Norman.

Inspired by his time with Jacques Cousteau, John wrote "Calypso," a huge hit for him in the mid-'70s. All proceeds of the song, which were substantial, went to the Cousteau Society. Photo courtesy John Denver photo archive.

APPENDIX

A Guide to the Music of John Denver

With Rush Evans

This book has been my way of documenting my own fascinating ride with a popular musician. It has also been a documentation of who the man was, and the imagery that accompanied the multifaceted life of my friend John as I knew him. It's an exploration behind the music. But it's my great hope (and I'm certain it was also John's) that the music of John Denver is what will continue to reach people, continue to resonate, and continue to inspire for many years to come.

We all know some of John's songs by heart, but there were hundreds more. There are many album titles even John Denver fans would not recognize, let alone own. To get the complete picture and scope of John's music, I think it's important to see the entire catalog, compiled for me here by my friend and music historian Rush Evans with some personal commentary by me.

The Mitchell Trio:
That's the Way It's Gonna Be (1965)

John first arrived in the recording world as the lucky winner in an audition to replace Chad Mitchell in the Chad Mitchell Trio (soon to become simply the Mitchell Trio, considering its namesake's absence). He'd been hanging out in the LA folk scene for a little while by then, having abandoned his previous pursuit of an architecture degree. In the mid-1960s, folk acts like this one, along with the Brothers Four, the Kingston Trio, and the New Christy Minstrels, were selling lots of records. They were satisfying the American audience that was disinterested in rock and roll, while capturing a portion of that genre's following as well (given their inclusion of social relevance and occasional political commentary in their music). The Mitchell Trio proudly continued carrying folk music's torch, particularly important after Bob Dylan's move from his acoustic roots to an electric sound. But these were clean-cut acts, the kind Mom and Dad could listen to, that dressed in sport coats while appearing on *The Mike Douglas Show*, and that could sing a real pretty song in harmony, all while working in an anti-war message.

This was the ninth album by the trio, but it was the first with John. He's laughing big on the cover, wearing a coat and tie, no glasses. He stood out in the tracks, too, as his distinctive voice broke through clearly in the mix with Joe Frazier and Mike Kobluk as they took on topical material like "Lucy Baines" and "I Was Not a Nazi Polka." There are also nice covers of "Get Together" and Dylan's "Mr. Tambourine Man." The trio's musical director was Milt Okun, who had already worked with Paul Robeson and many others. Milt got John the audition. If John and Milt hadn't first crossed paths through the Mitchell Trio, John's solo career would likely not have unfolded the way that it eventually did.

The Mitchell Trio: *Violets of Dawn* (1965)

John's second record with the trio included more topical political material like "Your Friendly, Neighborhood, Liberal Ku-Klux-Klan," several Tom Paxton covers (Paxton also wrote the liner notes), and a handful of more serious, thoughtful folk songs, like Eric Andersen's "Violets of Dawn" and Fred Neil's "Another Side of This Life." Another noteworthy songwriter contributed a tune called "For Bobbi," written for his girlfriend at the time. No one could tell yet that it was written by the newest member, as it was credited to John's real name, H. J. Deutschendorf Jr. It's a song John would sing the rest of his life [later renamed "For Baby (For Bobbie")] and a pretty great one to serve as a songwriter's first recorded track.

John Denver Sings (1966)

The Mitchell Trio also afforded John the opportunity to be not only a genuine recording and touring artist, but also to perform his own songs within the context of the group. A song that he called "Babe I Hate to Go" was memorable, melodic, and beautiful. It was a simple lyric of a man having to spend time away from the woman he loved, truly a slice of life from the pen of a traveling musician. But in 1967, it could sound only like the tale of a young soldier headed half a world away to fight in a controversial war in Vietnam.

With two Mitchell Trio records under his belt, John recorded his first album, but it's not what you think: He recorded *John Denver Sings* and privately pressed 250 copies for the sole purpose of sharing them with friends as a Christmas present. The record was an informal labor of love, but it really captured the solo artist yet to come. The voice was already there, and along with "Babe I Hate To Go," it included four lovely Beatles covers ("Here, There and Everywhere," "And I Love Her," "Yesterday," and "In My Life") along with nice versions of the Everly Brothers' "When Will I Be Loved" and Phil Ochs's "What's That I Hear."

This previously lost treasure wouldn't see proper release until well into the twenty-first century, as RCA included it in its massive box set of John's work during the RCA years. It can also be purchased online individually.

Many of those original 250 copies had gone to musicians John had met along the road as a member of the trio. "I gave a copy each to Peter, Paul, and Mary," he later said. "When they came to their first rehearsal after Christmas holidays to work on this new album, each one of them said, 'Hey, I got a new John Denver song we've gotta do,'" referencing "Babe I Hate to Go." They fell in love with the timely song and recorded it in 1967.

The Mitchell Trio: *Alive* (1967)

By the time of John's third and final album with the trio, "Babe I Hate to Go" had become, at Milt Okun's urging, "Leaving, on a Jet Plane." The comma after *Leaving* would soon disappear as the song went on to become, of course, a number one hit for Peter, Paul and Mary. But not yet. This live album would be the song's first wide release. And this time, John's original contributions were credited to John Denver, not Deutschendorf (his other original on this album was a novelty song called "Like to Deal with the Ladies"). Onstage banter is included, as was the timely material the trio had been known for, along with a lovely, harmonized version of the Beatles' "She Loves You."

By the way, Joe Frazier had been asked to leave the trio by Kobluk, replaced by Texan David Boise, leaving Mike Kobluk as the only remaining member from Chad's original lineup.

John Denver with the Mitchell Trio: *Beginnings* (1974)

This compilation included tracks from those first two Mitchell Trio albums (plus a previously unreleased studio version of "She Loves

You") as Mercury Records' opportunistic way to cash in on John's massive popularity by the mid-'70s. There he was, pictured all alone in a pretty cool artist's rendering on a record by a trio. It was stocked right there among all the real John Denver records in stores, and I imagine some people got it home before realizing it wasn't really a new record from John. The good news is that the tracks chosen feature John's voice prominently, and the Mitchell Trio material had held up well. "Leaving on a Jet Plane" was not included, as the *Alive* album had been released on Reprise Records; Mercury didn't have access to it.

The Mitchell Trio and Denver, Boise & Johnson: *Leaving on a Jet Plane* (2018)

When Kobluk left the Mitchell Trio, John was the last man standing and intent on keeping the trio going. Their new member was a fine singer-songwriter named Michael Johnson, and they were booked on *The Mike Douglas Show* as the New Mitchell Trio. But that didn't go anywhere because there were no longer any original members. The trio then became Denver, Boise & Johnson, releasing a handful of singles, gathered here for the first time in 2018, along with several other Mitchell Trio rarities.

The electric version of "Leaving on a Jet Plane" had also been released only as a single by the Mitchell Trio in 1967, and it's included here, giving a whole new Byrds-like feel to the song. Among the 1968 Denver, Boise & Johnson tracks are a topical swipe at a then presidential candidate called "'68 Nixon (This Year's Model)" and a then new Denver original called "Take Me to Tomorrow," another rocker that would soon enough be a title track for a solo album. Their sweet version of Joni Mitchell's "Both Sides Now" is released here for the first time, as is "Yellow Cat," sung by Boise here but a song that John wouldn't forget. Boise had presumably brought it from the burgeoning Texas folk scene, a Steven Fromholz song that John would also include on his first proper solo album. Johnson, by the way, went on to have a pretty major hit in the '70s with "Bluer Than Blue."

Rhymes & Reasons (1969)

With the demise of the various lineups of the trio, Milt Okun and John were ready to start making John Denver records. The procurement of a contract with RCA Records was a very big deal, and in those days, nurturing an artist and allowing him the time to grow was common-place. That's what RCA did for John, who had a two-year, four-album contract. The first album, *Rhymes & Reasons*, is arguably the finest of his early years. It included, of course, his own version of "Leaving on a Jet Plane," which displayed a poignancy and sincerity absent in Peter, Paul and Mary's widely heard hit. The song simply made better sense sung not by that trio or the one John had just come from but by a single voice—that of the man who was leaving on the jet plane.

And what better voice than that of its writer? John would prove with his voice that one need not display the raspy ruggedness of a Tom Waits, Neil Young, or even Bob Dylan to capture delicate feelings of uncertainty, passion, or sadness. John's voice provided a sound that was original, an unpretentious and straightforward vocal style in the true folk tradition, quite deliberately singing of "The Love of the Common People"—the cover song that opened the album. But his voice also owed a debt to the smooth styling of the classic crooners, perhaps the reason for its rigidity in these early recordings (it would relax into a more comfortable sound later).

Eleven of the album's fourteen tracks were covers, including little-known gems by Texas writers Mike Williams ("Catch Another Butterfly"), the aforementioned Steven Fromholz ("Yellow Cat"), and Jerry Jeff Walker ("My Old Man"). Even the Beatles' "When I'm

Sixty-Four" was in the mix. All fit well into the joyous and contemplative message John was already sharing.

It was clear right away that the bespectacled young man on the cover was earnest and committed to his celebration of life and nature. When singing "Today Is the First Day of the Rest of My Life," it was a sincere philosophical statement, not a clever cliché. "Catch Another Butterfly" was an adult reconnection with the meaning of life—not an innocuous kids' song. "I Wish I Knew How It Would Feel to Be Free" was a soulful interpretation of jazz artist Billy Taylor's and Dick Dallas's civil-rights anthem (previously recorded by Nina Simone).

No song in his eventually vast catalogue would capture John's simple point as succinctly as this first album's title song.

The words couldn't have been more heartfelt. "I was trying to define my beliefs as a man," he later wrote in his autobiography, *Take Me Home*. "What I thought life was about and for . . . Where those particular lyrics came from, I don't know. I can only guess."

Take Me to Tomorrow (1970)

John wrote six of the eleven tracks on his second solo record, including that title cut that had previously been a Denver, Boise & Johnson single. "Take Me to Tomorrow" was a rocker and a strong statement to open the record, which then progressively settled into the softer sound for which he would soon become known. Though the album produced no hits, this was where a few particularly meaningful originals first appeared, like the sweet love song "Follow Me" and "Aspenglow," his most explicit lyrical description of beauty in nature to that point. This hauntingly beautiful track was a sign of things to come.

James Taylor's sweet "Carolina in My Mind" was perfect for John, while Jacques Brel's "Amsterdam" was quite unusual, a dark tale of sailors on shore leave, soon to be covered also by David Bowie.

Whose Garden Was This (1970)

Released just five months after its predecessor, John's third solo album was similar to the second in that there was a similar feel in production and stylistic mixtures. None of the new original songs would become memorable fan favorites, and once again, there were no hits. It's still a good record, particularly with thoughtful covers of the Band's "The Night They Drove Old Dixie Down," Jerry Jeff Walker's "Mr. Bojangles," and the Beatles' "Eleanor Rigby."

Another Beatles song, "Golden Slumbers," figures into a medley with Paul Potash's "Tremble If You Must" and John's "Sweet Sweet Life." It's a lovely, ambitious trilogy that works, but still, not a hit in sight or anything that radio would embrace. John had three fine albums under his belt but only one more chance to continue as a major label recording artist.

Poems, Prayers & Promises (1971)

It was on this album that the poems, the prayers, the promises—the things that John believed in—would forever and always be set against vivid portrayals of nature. The titles of the songs said it all: "I Guess He'd Rather Be in Colorado," "Sunshine on My Shoulders," and of course, "Poems, Prayers and Promises." The covers fit right in thematically, like the Beatles' "Let It Be," Paul McCartney's "Junk" (included on McCartney's first solo record released just a year earlier), and James Taylor's "Fire and Rain." John's voice had come into its own by this time, a pristine sound to accompany such pretty songs. It shone most brightly on his own love song "My Sweet Lady."

But it was a cowrite that changed everything and became the turning point in John's career. And, like "Leaving on a Jet Plane," the original title had been changed prior to release, this time to avoid confusion with James Taylor's "Country Road." It was 1971, and again, the imagery of going home was accidentally identifiable with the hope for safe return of soldiers from a war so far away. But "Take Me Home, Country Roads" also painted a clear image of very real places, like the Blue Ridge Mountains and the Shenandoah River.

John saw this one coming, this song written with friends Bill Danoff and Taffy Nivert. Everything about it felt like a hit. "Bill brought out a song he had been working on, which he said he didn't seem to be able to go anywhere with. He hoped I might have some thoughts on what to do with it," remembered John in his autobiography *Take Me Home*.

"I wrote a bridge and maybe a second verse. That night, Taffy and Bill did their show, I did mine, and afterward, when I got an encore, I brought them onstage with me and we did the new song. The place went crazy."

Then the whole country went crazy, turning the difficult-to-categorize young man into an instant star. He didn't look or sound like a country-and-western performer, and neither did he fit in with the glittery and glamorous contemporary hit makers (the folk rockers who'd influenced him having already run their course in the limelight). This was not folk music, and it wasn't rock. It was something new—an earthy, celebratory pop.

Simultaneous to the making of this unlikely music star, the youth of America had become enamored with an equally original personality and creator of a sound different from any heard in popular music to date.

Only in the 1970s could the two most famous musicians have been somewhat nerdy looking guys with glasses. The musical statements and personal styles of John Denver and Elton John were worlds apart, just as their own backgrounds had been, but they shared one thing more than any other: an ability to write a pretty melody showcased by a beautiful voice. And in the early 1970s, those other differences were irrelevant anyway. It was okay to hear "Take

Vista of the valley below John Denver's property in Starwood. Photo courtesy Lowell Norman.

Me Home, Country Roads" on the radio right after "Crocodile Rock," and it was okay when the Carpenters were played next to a John Lennon song. The compartmentalized separation of music hadn't taken hold of the radio industry yet. Back then, a hit was a hit to be heard by everyone.

The two biggest up-and-coming stars of the decade had been settled on, and John was one of them.

Aerie (1971)

The fifth album, 1971's *Aerie*, continued spreading the positive message of the enigmatic musician. The sunset cover photo of a silhouetted John with an eagle perched on his arm captured what the record did: his most beautiful creation yet of environmental beauty and life, human and otherwise. As good as the whole record is, it produced no hits—even though it was the follow-up to a record featuring the first of John's two biggest hits and the predecessor to the record with the second hit.

This album brought a diverse collection of songs together, forming a cohesive piece, simple and glorious. John's originals in his newfound natural niche shared moments with a spirited re-creation of Buddy Holly's "Everyday," a mournful read of Kris Kristofferson's "Casey's Last Ride," and an impassioned version of Bill Danoff's anti-war tale "Readjustment Blues," as close as John would ever come to singing a protest song.

John also covered Steve Goodman's brilliant train song "City of New Orleans." John would later tell the story from the stage that he and Arlo Guthrie had both learned Goodman's song from its composer at the same time and joked he was ticked off that Arlo had beat him to the song, which became a hit. John's version on this album came out months ahead of Arlo's single, which makes one wonder why it hadn't been released as a single by John. Would it have become another huge hit for him? Maybe things worked out just right, as Arlo's version was great, too. Willie Nelson's 1984 version earned Steve Goodman a posthumous Grammy the following year.

John's own "Starwood in Aspen" and "All of My Memories" were among his more thoughtful pieces to date, and a new song written with Mike Taylor served as the centerpiece of the whole record. "The Eagle and the Hawk" was a two-minute gem with no chorus and a soaring vocal that would eventually become one of John's most beloved songs.

Rocky Mountain High (1972)

"I moved here to Colorado in the summer of my twenty-seventh year, and in that summer got reintroduced to camping," said John in a posthumous 1998 PBS documentary. It was a story I'd heard him tell in concerts and interviews a hundred times. "One of the great camping trips that we did that summer was during the period of the great Perseid meteor shower, August 12 to 15 every year. We'd had a great little campsite set up on this lake right at the tree line, and then pretty soon as we're laying there watching this sky, and there's a little shooting star there and one there, all of a sudden one was smoking all the way across the sky. I thought everybody was asleep, and you'd hear, 'Wow! Did you see that?' For me, it was raining fire in the sky. I really felt, it certainly strengthened my feeling, that I'd found a home for myself."

"Rocky Mountain High" was a pop masterpiece, an eloquent wall of sound unlike any popular song to date. It provided escapism for a society weary of its own anger, sadness, and disillusionment. But aside from all that, it was good. It was a rich, full recording, a great melody with a sweeping acoustic arrangement and grand vocals. It was a hymn to the mountains. The *Rocky Mountain High* album also included the first solo version of "For Baby (For Bobbie)" and "Goodbye Again," the sequel to "Leaving on a Jet Plane." And John finally got to the Beatles cover that seemed all along to have been written for him: "Mother Nature's Son."

Most of side two featured the ambitious five-song "Season Suite," each painting a musical portrait of a different season (plus an instrumental, "Late Winter, Early Spring"). Creating visual footage for live performances of the suite was part of my job with John during the early years.

Farewell Andromeda (1973)

This was the John Denver record that one of my roommate's owned, the one with the beautiful painting on the cover and the music that fired my imagination to sketch out visual images to accompany each track, all before I knew anything about the man who would soon be my boss and friend.

Farewell Andromeda featured several fine new songs, like the title track, the mournful "We Don't Live Here No More," and the sweeping opening cut "I'd Rather Be a Cowboy (Lady's Chains)." The strings and arrangements were led by Lee Holdridge, in his first record with John. A few months after this release, Lee's orchestral work could be heard as the musical foundation of Neil Diamond's *Jonathan Livingston Seagull* album.

This record is also notable for a few personal inclusions. Its inner jacket contained the first reference to John's interest in Werner Erhard's est, a program within the human potential movement of the time that significantly affected John's work. Also, the song "Zachary and Jennifer" spoke openly about the desire of John and Annie to become parents. After concluding they couldn't have children of their own, they would adopt the first of two kids a year after the album, and as the song promised, they would name him Zachary (daughter Anna Kate would come a few years later). I first heard this album in June 1973, having never been exposed to his music previously other than being aware of hits "Rocky Mountain High" and "Take Me Home, Country Roads." By September 1 of that same year, I would be flying to Ohio to work my first concert with him. Fate.

John Denver's Greatest Hits (1973)

Following up a record that produced no hits with a greatest-hits package for an artist with only two proper radio hits of his own was the brilliant brainchild of Jerry Weintraub. *John Denver's Greatest Hits* captured John and his sound perfectly. People bought it, and it shot to number one on the album charts. "Sunshine on My Shoulders," originally released over two years earlier, became its own runaway hit, reaching number one in early 1974.

John did his part to make the album both a commercial and artistic success. Ever the perfectionist and serious artist, John took the opportunity to make new recordings of seven of his earlier songs. The new versions were fresh and consistent with the sound of the actual hits.

Among those new recordings was "Leaving on a Jet Plane," now firmly entrenched as John's own song, not just that number one hit for Peter, Paul and Mary before anyone knew who he was. The new vocal on "Rhymes and Reasons" was more relaxed, more natural than the original. Later compilation albums include the original 1969 track, but this special version of one of the best songs John ever wrote resides solely on this record.

Here was forty minutes of joy, providing solace for an America exhausted from its years in Vietnam (a war in which John's own brother, Ron, had served) and from the drama and tragedy of the Watergate affair. It sold ten million copies in the first six months.

Instead of being a bunch of hits thrown together, it became a thoughtful musical statement of the songs that defined the artist. Greatest hits albums are usually a look back for major artists. In the case of John Denver, *Greatest Hits* was a fresh new look toward the future.

Back Home Again (1974)

The follow-up to *Greatest Hits* had more actual chart hits than its predecessor did! These include "Annie's Song," "Back Home Again," "Sweet Surrender," and "Thank God I'm a Country Boy." Even ones that weren't hits became some of John's most beloved songs over the course of his career, like "This Old Guitar," "The Music Is You," and the sweet, personal tribute to John's late Uncle Dean, who'd died at age twenty: "Matthew." This multiplatinum record also had a country feel, which got John radio play on the country stations.

And by the way, I took the cover photo and did the initial graphic design for this one—my first for John. It was fitting that Annie appears in the picture, since "Annie's Song" is on this record, but Annie had no interest in fame or recognition. She picked this photo over my protest, as I felt it was not a great shot of her. And she picked it for that very reason—so that no one would recognize her!

The album was printed in two ways. The brighter, crisper cover was the original, and I happened to be at John's house when he received the first copies in the mail. He opened the package up, and he said, "What do you think?" I said, "It's gaudy! It's way different from what we'd envisioned." John agreed. The colors were ridiculous, and it looked more like a carnival than the more old-fashioned photo album look that we'd originally conceived.

John picked up the phone right then and there and called Weintraub to tell him that he didn't like it. It was that simple. I remember thinking:

Wow, this is power right here. That's when you know you've made it, when all you have to do is call one guy, upsetting the entire production schedule to end up with what you wanted. The newer, softer cover was soon in production and in stores, and it felt more like the back-home concept that the whole record had been about in the first place.

An Evening with John Denver (1975)

Magic. The entire John Denver experience comes together in this two-record set. For me, of course, it's representative of so much of my job with John in those first several years. The gatefold inside cover photo shows the screens and their images behind the band, representing my contribution to the John Denver show at the time.

As a performance, it captured it all: John's humor and rapport with the audience, the band's stellar musicianship, and the excitement in the room for the moving event that was a John Denver concert. The recordings came from a week of shows at the Universal Amphiteatre in Universal City, California, before it was converted to a covered auditorium, but the album's consistent sound comes off like a single show. Lee Holdridge conducted the orchestra, and the strings really shine throughout.

There were plenty of hits by this time, and John performs them perfectly here, along with some great new covers for the set—most notably "Today" by John's old friend Randy Sparks, from the New Christy Minstrels, and "Boy from the Country" written by Michael Martin Murphey and Owens Castleman. Murphey had already made some great records with great songs, but he wouldn't have his first major hit until "Wildfire" in February 1975, the very month that this live set from John was released. John and Murphey would soon be friends, both managed by Jerry Weintraub, performing Murphey's "Carolina in the Pines" on *The Tonight Show* together later in the year. The excellent new original "Annie's Other Song" appeared only on this album.

When people talk about the best live albums ever released, they almost always mention *Frampton Comes Alive!* which came out one year after *An Evening with John Denver*. Both records stand together as lightning captured in a bottle on stage in California in the mid-'70s, documenting the times perfectly.

Windsong (1975)

As busy as we were at the time with concerts, television shows, and environmental film projects, I am still amazed that John could continue writing and recording so many beautiful songs at such an astounding pace. That's why we called him the "Adrenaline Kid." And somehow, *somehow*, he kept making excellent records, like *Windsong*.

John enjoyed his first two-sided hit with the lovely "I'm Sorry" and "Calypso," his tribute to the research ship of Jacques Cousteau, the French marine conservationist and explorer whom he had befriended. The song about the ship became yet another way in which John used his music to draw attention to conservation, and I'm certain that more people became aware of Cousteau's important work as a result of this song. John also gifted the royalties of the song to the Cousteau Society. Cousteau passed away at eighty-seven in 1997, just four months before John's death.

Just as close to John's heart as the preservation of the seas was his growing interest in Werner Erhard's est (Erhard Seminars Training), a program through which John was finding great personal development and self-improvement. The song "Looking for Space" was inspired by his est experience. "It's about looking for the definition of who you are, by finding out where you are, not only physically, but mentally and emotionally," he told *Billboard* magazine.

It was perfectly articulated introspection, just as "Rhymes and Reasons" had been. Much later, the song was played in its entirety in what was to have been the final four minutes of the hit television show *Magnum, P.I.*, but Tom Selleck would actually go on to play Magnum another year, so its usage wound up being part of a season-ending cliffhanger.

"Fly Away" was another great hit from *Windsong*, recorded as a duet with Olivia Newton-John, also at the height of her popularity. The thoughtful title song could've been yet another hit, had it been released as a single, and it's worth noting that it was a cowrite with Joe Henry, with whom John would write many more songs in the years to come. Joe is a brilliant songwriter and great guy; his contribution to John's body of work is meaningful and significant.

Rocky Mountain Christmas (1975)

One month after the release of "Windsong", John released his first Christmas album. It included two new versions of previously released songs: "Please, Daddy (Don't Get Drunk This Christmas)" and "Aspenglow", plus a great new single that became a minor Christmas hit, "Christmas for Cowboys," which had been written by John's guitarist Steve Weisberg. The rest of the album included Christmas classics like "Silver Bells," "Silent Night," and "The Christmas Song," all sung from the heart in the pristine voice of the most popular American singer of the time. John's accompanying television Christmas special (also called *Rocky Mountain Christmas*) featured special guests Steve Martin, Valerie Harper, and Olivia Newton-John. John's special musical relationship with Christmas was just getting started.

Spirit (1976)

John's incredible run on the pop charts was basically over by this time, but that inevitability did nothing to change his status as a major American artist and public figure. And he kept making records, good ones, like *Spirit*, which included "Like a Sad Song," a Top 40 pop hit and a number one adult contemporary hit. Bill Danoff's "Baby, You Look Good to Me Tonight" didn't make the Top 40, but it, too, was an adult contemporary hit. AC radio was beginning to emerge as a viable and important format where John's music would live comfortably for the rest of his career.

Banner hanging from the famous Budokan arena. Translation: "John Denver Concert of Love."
Photo courtesy Lowell Norman.

"Come and Let Me Look in Your Eyes" and "The Wings That Fly Us Home" were excellent cowrites with Joe Henry. Covers like the standard "Polka Dots and Moonbeams" and western swing classic "San Antonio Rose" were also great fun. Speaking of that Bob Wills tune, it's worth mentioning that, even though John Sommers played the fiddle on the recording, John did know how to play the fiddle, as he did on stage many times for "Thank God I'm a Country Boy" with backup fiddle by band member Danny Wheetman accompanying him.

Live in London (1976)

Live in London is an RCA release alright, but it didn't come out in the states. It would've been quite redundant anyway to the massively successful *An Evening with John Denver*, but this was a solid single-record set for the British audience. Fine versions of the hits again with the full band and strings, and it's especially nice to hear "Amsterdam" and "Spirit," neither of which was on the other live record.

I took the back cover photo of John on stage at the London Palladium from behind with the spotlight silhouetting John and his guitar.

John Denver's Greatest Hits, Volume 2 (1977)

This time, there were plenty of hits under his belt, but like the previous greatest hits package, John recorded new versions of some of the songs, again to great effect. Five of the twelve songs were new recordings, one of which was "My Sweet Lady," a song that had first come out in 1971 and again in '75 on the live album. This new version finally gave the love song a chance to be a hit, which it became when released as the single for this record.

Another unfortunate choice of cover photography, in my opinion. John hated the shot of himself, but I believe Weintraub pushed it through in such a rush that there was no time to change it.

I Want to Live (1977)

The title track of *I Want to Live* was John's composition designed to provide musical support and context to his important work with The Hunger Project. After seeing the film *The Hungry Planet*, John and fellow recording artist Harry Chapin approached President Jimmy Carter encouraging a Presidential Commission on World Hunger.

John envisioned "I Want to Live" as something of a theme song for the commission. It was all one musician's determination to draw attention to the devastation of hunger across our planet. In the following decade, Bob Geldof would inspire a musical movement that enlisted the help of major artists for his "Feed the World" recording, followed a year later by the "We Are the World" track and the massive Live Aid concerts. John was inexplicably excluded from all of these efforts, which mystifies me. For the record, once upon a time, a major performing artist named John Denver wrote a beautiful song about world hunger that everyone should hear.

My wife, Debbie, and I were visiting the guesthouse for a few days, and as we were driving into Aspen with John one afternoon in separate vehicles, he pulled us over to sing the opening lyrics to "I Want to Live" as it had just begun to form in his head. It was all there, the melody and the title lyrics. The verses would come later.

The rest of the album is beautiful, with three John originals released as singles: "How Can I Leave You Again?" "It Amazes Me," and "I Want to Live."

Tom Paxton's rich and mellow "Bet on the Blues" is a delightful departure for John, different from the kind of song he would write, but he turned in a fine version, one of many Tom Paxton covers he recorded over the years. Folk singer Eric Andersen's "Thirsty Boots" is also an excellent cover, and it's one that sounds like John could've written. Old friend Bill Danoff contributed a sweet love song called

"Dearest Esmeralda," masterfully supported by Lee Holdridge's orchestral arrangement.

John Denver (1979)

When you have one of the founding fathers of rock and roll guitar in the band, it's a good idea to let him show it, as James Burton does on John's version of "Johnny B. Goode," which works quite well. There are some other highlights on this one, very much including new originals like "You're So Beautiful," "Songs of . . . ," and the reflective "What's on Your Mind." John had released a version of Bryan Bowers's "Berkeley Woman" years earlier but felt strongly enough about the song that he included a new version here, the only live performance on the record. Herb Pedersen wrote a nice song on this one called "Southwind." David Mallett's "Garden Song" was covered by Arlo Guthrie, Paul Stookey, Pete Seeger, and many others. It works perfectly in John's sensitive take on the memorable song.

I took the cover photo of John at one of the concerts at Harrah's Lake Tahoe. It was not my pick. I went to Jerry Weintraub's office on a Saturday with a couple dozen selections of recent concert photos. There were other photos I felt were better qualified. Jerry did about two minutes of looking at all of them on a light table and pointed to this one and said, "That's it." I asked why that particular shot and he said, "Because there's a lot of movement, action in it. He looks passionate."

John Denver & the Muppets:
A Christmas Together (1979)

John's reputation as a family entertainer had long been established by this time, so his work with the Muppets was a perfect fit with delightful collaborative results.

The musical Christmas television special they made together deserved a soundtrack, and another classic Christmas album was born. John sings on nine of the thirteen tracks, one of which was with Rowlf the Dog (voice of Muppets creator Jim Henson), two of which John sang solo, and the rest of which included the whole Muppet cast. Henson was also the original voice of Kermit the Frog and so many others in the cast. Frank Oz was Miss Piggy, among others. Those guys were iconic with these timeless characters.

John's cowrite with Joe Henry, "A Baby Just Like You," had appeared on his previous Christmas album, revived here, still with the reference to his first child, Zachary. "Silent Night" and "We Wish You a Merry Christmas" work beautifully with John's voice and those of the Muppets, but it's one song in particular he sings alone on the record that is most special: "Noel: Christmas Eve, 1913." Lee Holdridge had set music to the words of Robert Bridges, the poet laureate of the United Kingdom from 1913 to 1930. John sang it beautifully.

Autograph (1980)

The 1980s had begun. Popular music had been evolving in different directions, with punk and new wave celebrating a tighter and tougher rock sound.

The new John Denver record for the new decade sounded bright, fresh, and at least a little different. Milt Okun was still at the helm as producer, the band was virtually the same group of players of many years at that point, and Lee Holdridge still brought the strings into the mix. It was still a John Denver record, but there were a few different arrangements, with a few full-blown country tunes and a little of the alto sax that had started turning up on adult contemporary songs of the time.

"Dancing with the Mountains" opened things up with a harder edge supporting John's consistent themes and vocal approach. Ruby Rakes's "How Mountain Girls Can Love" might just be the most country-sounding track John ever recorded, and he sounded great on it, not just with the trademark John Denver voice but with that of an authentic musician with country roots. "The Ballad of St. Anne's Reel" was another country outing, a straight-up fiddle tune.

Songwriter and recording artist Rodney Crowell was just at the beginning of a long and brilliant career, and John wisely chose to cover his beautiful "Song for the Life." As always, John had his own beautiful songs to bring to the table, most notably the title song, in which he articulates his disinterest in literal autographs, and seeing his songs as his personalized transcriptions for fans. It was a love letter to those who had joined him on his wild ride of the previous decade.

Some Days Are Diamonds (1981)

As recently as his previous album, John had recorded some great country songs, and, of course, some of his biggest hits had been rooted in traditional country. This time, it was a calculated move by Jerry Weintraub that John should make a contemporary country album, as the pop hits had dried up, and he might find a new audience.

The trouble was, John never wanted to be a country singer. He didn't want to be categorized. John felt pushed to make this record, which is why he spoke negatively in his autobiography of the whole experience. On some of the tracks, he even sounds like a hired singer with little heart in it. He also recorded it in Nashville, where he didn't feel especially welcomed or wanted. However, there are some real highlights here, like a studio version of Michael Martin Murphey's "Boy from the Country" and the great title cover "Some Days Are Diamonds," written by hit country songwriter Deena Kaye Rose.

It was released as a single, as was the Bobby Goldsboro song "The Cowboy and the Lady," which both Goldsboro and Dolly Parton had previously recorded as "The Cowboy and the Dandy." Neither was a hit for John, but one of his two new originals, "Sleepin' Alone," should have been. It was solid proof that John could write a real bona fide country song with heart.

Seasons of the Heart (1982)

It's an unusual cover photograph for John Denver, especially for an album with a title like *Seasons of the Heart*, but the image of John walking down steps into a cave mattered to him. It was a self-portrait, a photo John himself had taken in 1981 of his entry into Purple Dragon Cave, Hangzhou, China, a trip he had made solo after we had finished our second successful Japan tour. These were tough and heady days for John, with a separation from Annie, his father's passing, and his eventual breakup with his longtime manager. All these things weighed heavily on his heart.

One of this very serious album's best songs was also set in China, a new original called "Shanghai Breezes," which was released as a single, as was the title track. John wrote "What One Man Can Do" on Buckminster Fuller's eighty-fifth birthday. The author, futurist, inventor, and forward-thinking theorist had become a major influence on John's ongoing education about the world around him.

John did a nice job on the great Jesse Winchester's "Nothing but a Breeze," a perfect cover for him. But it was another new song of his own that he would declare the best song he'd ever written. Annie has said the same—that she believes "Perhaps Love" is even a better song than the one he named for her. A year before this album came out, John had found himself back on the radio, thanks to his duet with opera legend Plácido Domingo on this grand song on the nature of love itself. That version had appeared on Domingo's album of popular music, which included a version of "Annie's Song," on which John played guitar. John's longtime producer, Milt Okun, had produced the record, which is how John and Plácido had been brought together.

"Perhaps Love" had gotten to the heart of love, just as "Rocky Mountain High" had gotten to the heart of nature, and just as "Rhymes and Reasons" had gotten to the heart of understanding life. This version of "Perhaps Love," without Domingo, is just the man and the song for under two minutes. It's easily among the best things he ever did, and it's a version that has hardly been heard.

John Denver and the Muppets:
Rocky Mountain Holiday (1982)

John's second collaboration with Jim Henson's Muppets was also the result of another television special by the best-known family entertainers in the world. Country favorites like "Tumbling Tumbleweeds"/"Happy Trails" and "Home on the Range" are great fun, as are new versions of some of John's hits, like "Poems, Prayers and Promises" and "Grandma's Feather Bed," the latter sung primarily by Kermit the Frog.

What's extra cool here is that John brought two new originals to the project: "Durango Mountain Caballero," which he sings alone, and "Hey Old Pal," which he sings with Kermit, Fozzie Bear, and the other Muppets. John's new version of Mike Williams's "Catch Another Butterfly" was also a perfect fit for this kid-friendly project.

Rocky Mountain Holiday was nominated for a Grammy Award for Best Recording for Children, but it lost to Michael Jackson's *E.T. the Extra-Terrestrial* storybook album. Still no Grammys for John Denver.

It's About Time (1983)

John was experiencing great personal change around this time, with the sudden and unexpected death of his father, Dutch (to whom *It's About Time* is dedicated), and the end of his marriage to Annie. He looked like a new man in the cover photo, with no trademark granny glasses, shorter hair, and a dapper white suit. He tried some new things musically, too, including smoother pop arrangements with Jim Horn's saxophone getting more airtime than acoustic guitar.

"Falling Out of Love" was right where John was, a sadly beautiful song documenting what was going on for him.

Great pain has always produced great art, it seems.

The opening track, "Hold on Tightly," and "World Game" were both straight-up reggae songs—good ones—featuring Bob Marley's widow, Rita, and reggae legend Marcia Griffiths on backing vocals. R&B singer Patti Austin also sings on the album, but it's a duet with Emmylou Harris that really stands out. "Wild Montana Skies" was an acoustic-based story song in the spirit of "Matthew" and one of John's most melodic and classic songs.

John's longtime friend and one of his tour managers, Barney Wyckoff, produced.

Greatest Hits Volume 3 (1984)

This was a nice overview of John's work from the late '70s through the early '80s—and an opportunity to get the duet with Plácido Domingo onto one of John's own records. On those first two greatest hits packages, John had recorded new versions of some of the songs. He didn't do that this time, but he did still bring new material to the project by way of two new songs, "The Gold and Beyond" and "Love Again," the latter sung with French Bulgarian singer Sylvie Vartan.

Dreamland Express (1985)

As the film noir–style cover photograph of a pensive John indicates, *Dreamland Express* represents a significant stylistic shift, the most dramatic of his career. He had been an adult contemporary artist for some time by 1985, but here he embraces the pop rock side of the format.

"The Harder They Fall" was an original that demonstrated a harder rocking edge than he would ever have, as did his cover of Roy Orbison's "Claudette." The title cut also took on the new sound but as a more medium-tempo ballad.

John's version of "Got My Heart Set on You" (written by Dobie Gray and Bud Reneau) was the first to be recorded, and it would be a country hit the following year by country singer John Conlee. By this time, the aptly named Jim Horn's contribution of horns to John's work was popping up frequently. On "If Ever," Jim's saxophone is heard trading solos with the distinctive harmonica of Stevie Wonder, who also cowrote the song.

"Don't Close Your Eyes Tonight" fully embraced the sound of romantic '80s pop, and like the title cut, was released as a single. It would also become a music video for VH1.

One World (1986)

"Flying for Me" is the majestic highlight of John's final record with RCA, with whom he had made musical history over the seventeen years prior. Milt Okun and Roger Nichols as producers returned John to his trademark sound for that track, but like the previous album, there were more stylistic departures as well, such as Danny O'Keefe and Bill Braun's gently rocking "Along for the Ride ('56 T-Bird)" and the new original title cut performed in the style of reggae.

For his last ever RCA-released song, John closed the record with one of his big-picture aspirations, "It's a Possibility." He would soon be a man without the support of a major label, but he wouldn't let that get in the way of his creation and release of new material.

Higher Ground (1988)

John Denver had spent the better part of two decades with RCA Records, but by this time, he was not, so he started his own label. His first outing on Windstar Records was this often overlooked, now hard-to-find album. "For You" was a great piano-based love song, "All This Joy" a beautiful hymn, and "Whispering Jesse" an outstanding ballad set again in the mountains and featuring vocals with his new wife, Cassandra. John wrote "A Country Girl in Paris" for Cassie, who also appeared in the music video.

The title song, written with Joe Henry and Lee Holdridge, served as the opening theme song for a television movie that John had starred in the same year, also titled *Higher Ground*.

Earth Songs (1990)

Earth Songs was another example of John being ahead of his time, this time in the business sense. And artistically speaking, it's also a fantastic album.

His second Windstar Records venture wasn't even released for wide distribution, available instead as a merch item at concerts and special order through the fan clubs. No longer a major-label recording artist, John could now sell a concept album like this at shows, and he didn't have to share profits with his former label. It was a scrappy move for a one-time major-label act determined to continue with his recording career.

Earth Songs included new recordings of nature-themed songs, most of which had been hits, some of which were deep cuts. Several new tracks were included as well. John's more mature voice worked well in the remakes, several of which, like "The Eagle and the Hawk" and "Calypso," featured an ethereal vocal echo effect not found in the originals.

Since this release, other artists have released albums just for sale at shows, for which they can keep all the proceeds. Maybe this trend has created a better environment for independent artists, giving them more control over their own songs and recordings. Texas singer-songwriter Terri Hendrix, for instance, has released several dozen albums on her own label, controlling the supply and all aspects of creativity, unbound by the major-label system in place during John's years.

John, the author, and Joan Holmes, president of The Hunger Project and our boss on our Africa trip. Photo courtesy John Denver photo archive.

The Flower That Shattered the Stone (1990)

I did the album design and art direction for this one, working with photographer Janel Pahl on the cover. It was an artful photo that tied beautifully into the title.

The Flower That Shattered the Stone has an interesting release history. A different version was first released a year earlier in Australia as *Stonehaven Sunrise*. This version consists of most of that record, plus two tracks from the previous *Earth Songs* album, presumably included because he wanted them in wider release (as *Earth Songs* had not been available in stores). The final song was an alternate version of the beautiful title track but sung with Kosetsu Minami, the Japanese folk singer who had become his friend. That track had been released earlier as a single in Japan.

Along with the title track written by Joe Henry and John Jarvis, "Thanks To You," "The Gift You Are," and the majestic "Eagles and Horses" are highlights. John's version of the great Jimmy Webb's "Postcard from Paris," for which I created a music video, is also included. One song that didn't migrate from that Australian version over to this one was "And So it Goes," a version of which had been originally recorded with the Nitty Gritty Dirt Band and included on their *Will the Circle Be Unbroken, Volume Two* album. When the Dirt Band appeared on public television's *Austin City Limits*, they brought in John to sing the song, along with spirited versions of "Take Me Home, Country Roads" and "Rocky Mountain High" that also included Michael Martin Murphey, New Grass Revival, the Carter Sisters, Paulette Carlson of Highway 101, and bluegrass legends Vassar Clements and Jimmy Martin.

By the way, Olivia Newton-John told us about her own connection to the lyrics of the title song: "Joe Henry was a very dear friend of John's, and he wrote a lot of lyrics for John's songs. He cowrote 'The Flower That Shattered the Stone.' He wrote the lyrics to that for one of my best friends who lost her daughter, Colette, to cancer."

Christmas Like a Lullaby (1990)

Counting the one with the Muppets, this was John's third Christmas album, but this time on his own Windstar Records. He finally got to the Christmas classics he hadn't yet covered, like "White Christmas." The whole thing is beautiful and classic John.

The album was reissued by Delta Music/LaserLight Digital later, and this is the copy with a closeup of John in front of the field of snow-covered trees, which can be much more commonly found. This version includes John's special take on music educator and historian Jester Hairston's "Mary's Boy Child," first made famous by Harry Belafonte.

Different Directions (1991)

A great return to form in this last Windstar Records outing, supported by the core band of many years: James Burton, Jerry Scheff, Glen D. Hardin, and Jim Horn. John produced it himself, and highlights include Bill Danoff's "Potter's Wheel" and Jeffrey Hawthorne Bullock's "Ponies." John's own nine-minute epic "The Foxfire Suite" is reminiscent, in form anyway, of the early "Season Suite," and finds John at his aspirational best as a songwriter.

The same goes for "Amazon (Let This Be a Voice)," in which John gives a voice to the mountains, the river, the forest, the flowers, the ocean, the desert, the children, and the dreamers, and intones, "Let this be a voice of no regret."

John thanked Chip Davis for his influenc e on this album, as the two friends were spending a lot of time together around then. This album was produced at Davis's studio in Omaha, Nebraska. Davis had already made a series of New Age records with Mannheim Steamroller, and would go on to produce an annual high-production touring Christmas road show with that group.

I took the photos and created the design for the entire package and was pleased with how it came out. As it turned out, it would be my last package design. I created a music video for "Potters Wheel" from this album, as well. Like the rest of the Windstar material, I wish this album could be more widely known.

The Wildlife Concert (1995)

Once again, the stage proved to be the best medium John Denver had ever had for sharing his rhymes and reasons. Also released as a performance video, *The Wildlife Concert* reminded everyone who saw it on public television just how good John was as a performer and what a singular talent he remained. It also marked his return to a major label, and this time it was Sony.

This was first released as a two-CD set. It was later reissued with just sixteen of the original twenty-eight tracks as the single CD *The Best of John Denver Live*.

Love Again (1996)

The greatest hits are newly recorded again as *Love Again*, this time on independent record label CMC International. The new versions sounded great with John's more mature voice across the sixteen tracks. Sometimes called *The Unplugged Collection*, it would also be reissued posthumously with just twelve of the tracks as *A Celebration of Life (1943–1997)*.

Mighty Day: The Chad Mitchell Trio Reunion (1994; Recorded in 1987)

Though it was not released until 1994, this reunion concert by the original Chad Mitchell Trio had actually occurred in 1987 and aired as a PBS television special in 1992. The trio had been a huge success on the college circuit, but their recordings had been long out of print. Chad Mitchell, Joe Frazier, and Mike Kobluk perform thirteen of the fifteen tracks included together, and then John Denver comes out to thank Chad for having left the group back in the '60s. Would we have ever heard of John if he hadn't? John then performs a lovely version of "For Baby (For Bobbie)" with Frazier and Kobluk, the trio as it had existed after Mitchell's departure. Then all four vocalists sing "Last Night I Had the Strangest Dream" together. It's a delightful collector's item for John Denver purists, and the tracks sound great.

All Aboard! (1997)

Marketed as a kids' record, *All Aboard!* was a concept album filled with some of the greatest train songs ever written, like Utah Phillips's "Daddy, What's a Train?," Curtis Mayfield's "People Get Ready," Jimmie Rodgers's "Waiting for a Train," Lead Belly's "Lining Track," the traditional "I've Been Working on the Railroad," and John's new take on Steve Goodman's "City of New Orleans."

With this great new collection of songs once again on Sony, he was poised to make more high-profile records. It was released on August 26, 1997. John died fewer than two months later.

All Aboard! finally landed him a posthumous Grammy: Best Musical Album for Children. John's daughter Jesse Belle accepted the award for her father on the same Grammy Awards stage that her father had stood on to host the Grammys six times.

Forever, John (1998)

A year after John's death, RCA released this collection of rarities from its vaults, and it's hard to believe that fine tracks like "On the Wings of an Eagle," "River," and John's pristine take on the folk classic "Four

Strong Winds" had remained unreleased for years. John had several times recorded songs by brilliant Texas writers Guy Clark and Jerry Jeff Walker, both of whom are once again represented here in Guy's country classic "Rita Ballou" and an alternate take on Jerry Jeff's timeless "Mr. Bojangles."

The tracks had been recorded between 1969 and 1980. John was at his best during those years, and *Forever, John* feels like a fully realized studio album unto itself.

Live at the Sydney Opera House (1999; Recorded in 1977)

An earlier version of this live performance was released in Australia, the country in which it had been recorded on November 22, 1977, at the time that *I Want to Live* was John's newest album. All in all, it's another outstanding live performance from John and the band. Three tracks are included that weren't on the original Australian release, one of which—John Phillips's "Me and My Uncle"—had never appeared on a John Denver record.

"It's a Sin to Tell a Lie" is a delightful inclusion, which John follows up with a story about it being his mother's favorite song. He said he once performed it at Carnegie Hall in New York City with his parents in attendance. "Did that song and dedicated it to my mom . . . freaked her out!" he tells the audience Down Under.

A customized inclusion for the Australian audience is that country's folk ballad "Moreton Bay," pulled off nicely with just John and his guitar.

Christmas in Concert (2001; Recorded in 1996)

What a special documentation of a very different kind of John Denver concert. Recorded over two nights—December 19 and 20, 1996, at the DAR Constitution Hall in Washington, D.C.—*Christmas in Concert* is just that, made all the more beautiful by the presence of a Christmastime audience.

The World Children's Choir brought even more beauty, sounding magical with John's voice on "Away in a Manger," "Jingle Bells," and an incredibly stirring "Silent Night." Several non-Christmas hits are also included: "Take Me Home, Country Roads," "Annie's Song," and "Calypso."

Live in the USSR (2007; Recorded in 1985)

Here's a recording you will scarcely find in even the most esoteric record shops. In 1985, John was the first Western artist to perform in more than six years in what was then still the Soviet Union. The audience was quiet and didn't speak English, but John's natural charisma broke through in this stunning solo performance.

As John's only released solo performance, this little-known double album just might arguably be his best. John's mother contributed to the liner notes, and she declared it as her favorite. John's only sibling, Ron Deutschendorf, put it together and saw to its release. I can't think of a better body of music than John's for use in cultivating international diplomacy.

All of My Memories:
The John Denver Collection (2014)

A fitting title to include last. If you own only one John Denver album, this is the one to have. There are many other compilations, singles, double albums, even another four-disc set like this one, but this one goes beyond just the RCA material. The Mitchell Trio, as well as Denver, Boise & Johnson, are represented, as are rarities like a track with the Nitty Gritty Dirt Band, plus a few previously unreleased gems from the beginning of John's career, along with some alternate takes of familiar songs.

Those are the extras. The rest is filled with all the most beloved songs of the unique talent that was John Denver.

We need John's music now. He would undoubtedly have something to say about our imperiled planet. John had weighed in on the subject for the entirety of his musical career, articulated best in the lines of his signature song, "Rocky Mountain High."

John's personality illuminated his songs, songs that celebrated life and love. In those songs, we still have him and his message. "Nature is my first and best friend," he often said. If any musician ever connected personally with our natural world, and then translated that connection into the universal language of music, it was John Denver. He found serenity in the world, and then he shared it in song. His refreshing idealism was focused entirely on the big picture, the reasons for life and its beauty.

Aspen trees in early fall. Photo courtesy Lowell Norman.

ACKNOWLEDGMENTS

The writing of this book was a long and often lonely process. Without the kindness, gentle prodding, and occasional critiquing of friends, I'm quite sure these memories would still be locked away inside by head. So to the following, I offer my sincerest appreciation:

Robyn Baugher, whose continual push, honest critiquing, and positive energy kept my fingers on the keyboard for the two years it took to complete the process. Her faith in me and my story never wavered and provided all the inspiration I needed to carry on.

Barney Wyckoff, fellow traveler with me on the Rocky Mountain Highway, who often helped keep the story real with memories I had long since locked away.

John Sommers, Steve Voudouris, and Ron Lemire, other fellow travelers whose memory for technical details was of great assistance.

Tyler Norman, whose command of the English language helped pull me out of some writing corners and whose command of Photoshop helped in the tedious process of bringing back to life many faded and scratched photos.

Hal Blaine, whose friendly encouragement and experience writing his own memoir of his days with the Wrecking Crew were of great help.

Paul Arganbright and Tami Takahashi who gave my manuscript some early polishing.

Donna Kozik, who generously gave of her time and resources to get my manuscript seen. Her considerable talent in promoting new authors was the reason this book is now in your hands.

My agent, Leslie York of Fredrica S. Friedman & Co., for not only believing in me, but also that my story needed to be told.

Edward Ash-Milby, executive editor at Weldon Owen, whose energy and guidance through the publishing process has been of tremendous help.

And to Rush Evans, music aficionado extraordinaire, who first gave me the idea for this book by writing a brilliant essay about John in a trade magazine called *Goldmine*. His tireless research and energy in the first months of this exercise, and the countless edits and patience in the process, ended up giving me a voice I didn't know I had.

John as Deputy Dewey Cobb from one of his first acting gigs, an episode of *McCloud* with Dennis Weaver. Photo courtesy John Denver photo achive.

ABOUT THE AUTHORS

Lowell Norman

Lowell Norman was the videographer for John Denver for twenty-five years. He produced several music videos and documentary films for the artist's nonprofit Windstar Foundation. Norman's coproduction and direction of the hunger documentary *I Want to Live* was lauded as a landmark cinematic presentation about the politics of hunger. He lives in Lake San Marcos in northern San Diego County.

Rush Evans

Based in Austin, Texas, Rush Evans is a music journalist and longtime contributor to *Goldmine* magazine, a record collectors' publication. He hosts two radio programs at Austin's KOOP-FM: *Off the Beatle Path* and *The Singer and the Song*, a weekly live performance platform for singer-songwriters.

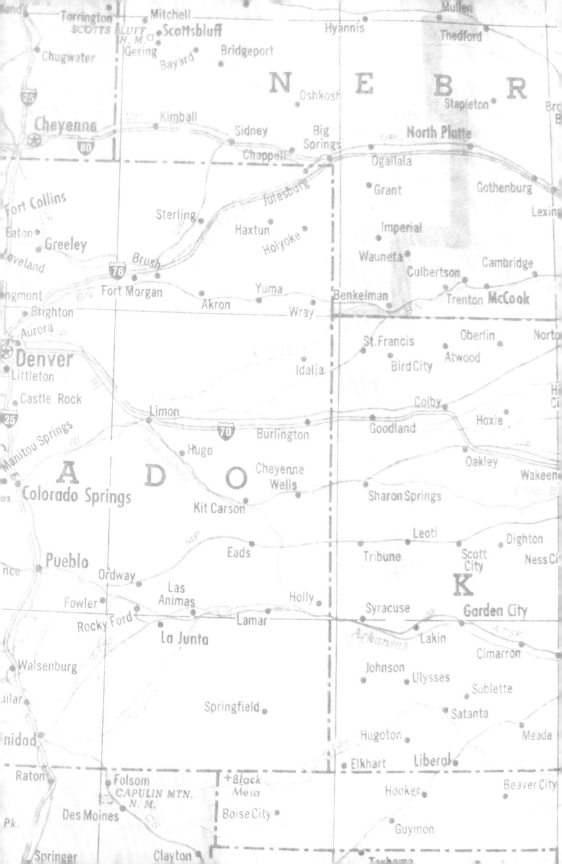

weldon**owen**

an imprint of Insight Editions
P.O. Box 3088
San Rafael, CA 94912
www.weldonowen.com

CEO Raoul Goff
VP Publisher Roger Shaw
Publishing Director Katie Killebrew
Executive Editor Edward Ash-Milby
VP, Creative Director Chrissy Kwasnik
Art Director Ashley Quackenbush
Senior Designer Stephanie Odeh
VP Manufacturing Alix Nicholaeff
Senior Production Manager Joshua Smith
Senior Production Manager, Subsidiary Rights Lina s Palma-Temena

Weldon Owen would also like to thank Bob Cooper.

The stories in this book reflect the author's recollection of events. Some names, locations,
and identifying characteristics have been changed to protect the privacy of those depicted.
Dialogue has been re-created from memory.

ISBN: 979-8-88674-110-0

Manufactured in China by Insight Editions
10 9 8 7 6 5 4 3 2 1

ROOTS of PEACE   REPLANTED PAPER

Insight Editions, in association with Roots of Peace, will plant two trees for each tree used in the manufacturing of
this book. Roots of Peace is an internationally renowned humanitarian organization dedicated to eradicating land
mines worldwide and converting war-torn lands into productive farms and wildlife habitats. Roots of Peace will
plant two million fruit and nut trees in Afghanistan and provide farmers there with the skills and support necessary
for sustainable land use.

Rawlins

Wheatland

Torrington
Mitchell
SCOTTS BLUFF
Scottsbluff
N.M.

Chugwater
Gering
Bayard
Br

MEDICINE BOW MTS.

Saratoga

Laramie

Cheyenne
Kimball
80
U.P.

Baggs

Walden

ROCKY
MTN.
NATIONAL
PK.

Fort Collins
Sterling

Craig
Steamboat
Springs
Estes Park
Eaton
Greeley
Brush
76

Maybell
Oak Creek
Longs
Pk.
Loveland
Fort Morgan
Akron

Kremmling
Hot
Sulphur Sprs.
Moffat Tunnel
Longmont
Brighton

Glenwood
Springs
Wolcott
Berthoud
Pass
Boulder
Aurora

Rifle
Eagle
Central City
Golden
Denver

Colorado
GRAND MESA
SAWATCH MTS.
Mt. Evans
Littleton

AND MESA
Breckenridge
Castle Rock
Limon

Mt. Elbert
Climax
70

Aspen
Leadville
Manitou Springs
Hugo

tion
Castle
Peak
Mt. Harvard
Fairplay

Paonia
O
L
O
R
A
D
O

BLACK CANYON
OF THE
GUNNISON
N.M.
Buena Vista
FLORISSANT
FOSSIL BEDS N.M.
Cripple Creek
Pikes
Pk.
Colorado Springs
Kit Cars

Gunnison
Gunnison
Canon
City
Kit Carson

Salida
SANGRE
Florence
Pueblo

Uncompahgre
Pk.
Saguache
Ordway

Ouray
Westcliffe
Fowler
Las
Animas

Silverton
Creede
GREAT SAND
DUNES N.M.
Rocky Ford

Del Norte
Center
Huerfano
La Junta

SAN JUAN
MTS.
Rio Grande
Blanca
Pk.
Walsenburg
Sprin

Monte Vista
Summit
Pk.
Alamosa
Aguilar

Pagosa
Springs
San Luis
DE
CRISTO
Trinidad

ango
Antonito

Chama
Raton
Folsom
CAPULIN MTN.
N.M.

Tierra
Amarilla
Questa
Wheeler Pk.
Des Moines

Taos
Pueblo
Cimarron
Springer
Clayton